Champagne

D1208108

KRUG
REIMS

PRODUCE OF FRANCE

Krug
House of Champagne

Krug
House of Champagne

by John Arlott

ILLUSTRATIONS BY TIMOTHY JAQUES

Davis-Poynter London

First published in 1976 by
Davis-Poynter Limited 20 Garrick Street London WC2E 9BJ

ISBN 0 7067 0199 2

Designed by Timothy Jaques FSIA and Gillian Greenwood

Filmset and printed in Great Britain by BAS Printers Limited, Wallop, Hampshire

To the family,
the wine and the tradition
called Krug

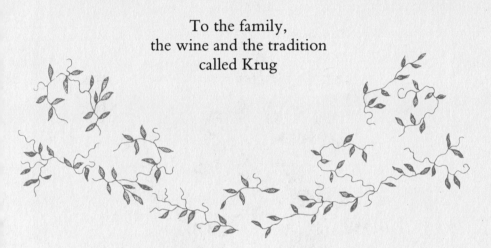

Contents

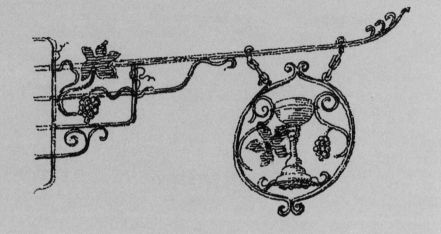

I

The facets of champagne

This is a book about an illustrious champagne. Yet, although it is an esteemed *grande marque*, it cannot exist in isolation, but only within all Champagne – a concept of many facets.

Champagne is, supremely, an idea. In languages far remote from French, people who have never seen – leave alone tasted – the wine of Champagne, use the word as an image of gaiety. In Lurçat's 'Song of the World' tapestry, 'Champagne', the grapes and vine roots – against a black background – burst from a barrel with beams, butterflies, blooms and branches in a blaze of brilliance. A schoolgirl said of her first glass 'It's like icicles of rainbow in my mouth'. Talleyrand called it 'The great civilizer'. 'Here, here, Master, see how it puns and quibbles in the glass' says Farquhar's character, Club. For Art Buchwald 'It tastes as if my foot has gone to sleep'. Its quick streamers of bubbles, racing through their golden prison out into the world make it the most visually exciting of all wines. To some it is a symbol of luxury or extravagance. It is pre-eminently the wine of celebration: and the finest *apéritif* ever conceived by man or provided by nature.

Originally, Champagne ('the Land of Plains') was the province of the Counts of Champagne, bounded on the north by Belgium and Luxembourg, on the west by the Ile de France and Picardy, to the south by Burgundy and the east by Lorraine. In 1790 it was divided between the *départements* of Ardennes, Marne, Haute Marne and Aube, and into parts of Seine-et-Marne, Aisne, Yonne and Meuse. It is a huge area – some 27,000 square miles – but, bled by Paris and largely given over to agriculture and woodland, its population is only about $1\frac{1}{4}$ million.

Many people – most of them French, but many British, American and German – still remember Champagne – though perhaps not by that name – as the battle-ravaged terrain over which the armies of centuries, from Ghengis Khan to Hitler, have advanced from the east on Paris. A Frenchman will point to a copse a few yards off some unremarkable strip of road near Chemin des Dames and say 'A thousand men died there in a day in 1917.' It was the field on which the First World War was won and lost. By 3 September 1914 the Germans were in Reims; by the 7 September they were across the Marne. This was the last line of defence for Paris and for four dreadful years dogged, savage battles were fought there. A single stone marks the centre of an area where five villages were so shattered by the interminable artillery bombardment and trench warfare that it would have been desecration to attempt to rebuild them. Memorials recall the French, British, Commonwealth, American, Moroccan, Russian and German troops who died there. The first battles that checked the German advance were waged among the grapes ripening for the 1914 vintage in vineyards some of which were so pulverised by weight of shell-fire that they have still not recovered. By May 1940 the Germans were back into France, again by way of Champagne, and this time they clung on until 1945, first as a demanding army of occupation and finally as a malevolent rearguard.

To the world in general, though, champagne is the wine and the district – much smaller than the ancient province – that produces it. That is a square of about forty miles north-south from the Aisne above Reims to the N33 and, east-west, between Châlons-sur-Marne and Dormans. It is in every way – topographically, geologically, viticulturally, scenically, socially and historically – the most interesting part of the otherwise monotonous plain of Champagne *pouilleuse*. Some millions of years ago a violent paroxysm of the earth's seething interior forced up a series of bluffs in the centre of that area. Crucially, the minute marine fossils which, as a result, became the effective growing soil of these hills, are formed of belemite chalk and – secondarily – chalk with fossilized micasters (sea urchins). The 25,000 scattered acres of these soils are ideal for the propagation of the grapes which, combined, create the greatest of all sparkling wines.

The axes of this little kingdom – *la Champagne viticole* – are Reims and Epernay; contrasting in every way; rivals yet united in the common cause of their wine. Reims is dominated physically – and all the champagne area spiritually – by the great cathedral. Gravely damaged by German bombardment during the First World War, it has been faithfully restored. Every day work is in progress on the prodigious tracery of its stonework. Every day pilgrims, trippers, sightseers, students come to visit it, to spend their minutes or hours in wonder and go on their way with a new experience implanted in their consciousness. Reims has largely recovered from its series of batterings. New industries have stabilised its economy and produced fresh growth. The nearness of Paris precludes it from reaching such size or influence as Marseilles, Toulouse or Bordeaux; but with a population of about 180,000 it is sixteenth in size of the provincial cities in France; and its prosperity is clearly to be seen.

Epernay, the other major champagne town, is smaller than Reims – about a sixth of the size – and even more closely involved with champagne. Creditably for a route town, it maintains a civilised tempo. The Avenue de Champagne, an amazing architectural extravaganza – with an occasional triumph like the French garden and the orangery Jean Baptiste Isabey designed – presents the palaces of the nineteenth-century champagne princes in an elaborate and successful publicity frontage. There is, too, in the Place de la République, a dramatically simple memorial stone to the dead of the Resistance: an urn set in concrete bears the names of Auschwitz, Buchenwald, Dachau, Mauthausen and Ravensbrück. Less tragic is a Parc de Maigret; a generous Rue de Reims (Reims replies with an Avenue Epernay), and the excellent champagne museum and library.

Smallest of the champagne towns, and the most completely committed to the wine, is Ay – strictly, Ay-Champagne – set among vineyard terraces; trees and vines lapping up to its walls; its generous church spire hoist high above the huddle of houses and close streets. In the sixteenth century not only the kings of France but Henry IV (proud to call himself Lord d'Ay) and Henry VIII of England, Charles V of Spain and Pope Leo X all owned vineyards there. The scale of prices for the *crus* of champagne used to be based upon the 100 per cent of Ay. Its population is still less than 8,000 but it is mightily busy and it sustains a number of champagne houses, outstandingly, of course, Bollinger; but also Ayala and Deutz et Gelderman.

Châlons-sur-Marne, substantially larger with a population of 54,000 and good communications, competed actively with Reims and Epernay for the champagne market in the early nineteenth century. Indeed, Joseph Krug, founder of the family business, entered the trade there. Gradually, however, the town became more deeply involved with other activities and now has a bare half-dozen *marques*, only Joseph Perrier of appreciable stature.

Champagne is too, a people, the *Champenois*. There are, of course, some ancient families among them but, in the main, they are the mixed race to be expected in a region which has been one of the main European highways of commerce, armies and ideas for more than two thousand years. They are largely a peasant people, less extrovert, less bibulous than those of most French wine regions: shrewd, quiet, notably industrious. They have been constantly under attack, much on the defensive; and have always proved resistant and resilient. In 1911 at Ay, though, growers from the Marne vineyards attacked and wrecked the cellars of makers they suspected of using grapes from outside the area in their champagne. So effective was their ferocity that the dragoons stood by reluctant to interfere, as the streets swam with champagne. The Government soon accepted their arguments to the extent of over-ruling the senate on a bill to control champagne-making. Subsequently, too, official excise returns confirmed their suspicions.

The *Champenois* tend often to drink still wine. Formerly, of course, there was a considerable production of still wine in the region: a white *Coteaux Champenois* (formerly *Vin Nature de Champagne*) and the long-established red Bouzy can be bought nowadays. Some growers make still wine for their own domestic use – though the controls are strict – and an appreciable amount of *vin ordinaire* is imported. Despite erosion by standardization, the *Champenois* retain a number of dialect words ('*parler champenois*'), many of them connected with drinking or the table – '*c'est ta fête, c'est toi qu'arroses*' (It's your treat – your turn to buy a round'); '*godailler*' is to go on a café- (or, in English, a pub-) crawl; '*cul-net*', to drink down in one gulp; three expressions for a drunk are '*churleur*', '*rondibus*' and '*sac-à-vin*'. Among the best of these terms are '*jus de chapeau*' for bad coffee; '*machoiller*' – almost impossible in English – to eat without appetite; '*couleuse*' is an important, though sad, *Champenois* expression for a bottle that has lost its gas – and some of its wine: and, best of all as a final note, '*luter*' is to drink well. Thus the *Champenois*, if not over-vocal, can be individually expressive.

They have, too, established a coherent and definable gastronomic character. The visitor does not merely drink the local wine; he eats the local dishes. The most famous of them is the *potée Champenoise*, a multi-meat casserole as vastly satisfying in impact as a Languedoc *cassoulet*. It is defensibly claimed, though, that the *matelote* (fresh fish stew) of Champagne is the finest of all in France. The Montagne de Reims may seem little more than a hillock to some from high mountain country, but there are still wild boar in the woods that cap it and the young (*marcassin*) are a cook's delight. Salmon poached in (still) champagne is incomparable; chicken similarly prepared and served with a fresh, utterly dry, sparkling champagne, is a memorable dish. Breaded and grilled pigs' trotters (*à la Saint-Ménehould*) is perhaps the unique dish of the region. Boursault cheese; *pâté de grives* (made from thrushes); *jambon de Reims*; *andouillettes* (sheep's-giblet sausages); and *salade au lard* (with dandelions, potatoes and vinegar), too, are specialities of the district, found in most of its restaurants. The *biscuit de Reims* is made to be 'dunked' in champagne. Monsieur Boyer's *La Chaumière* restaurant in Reims and the *Hostelerie du Château* at Fère en Tardenois, (forty-six kilometres towards Paris) have two stars in the *Michelin*; the *Royal Champagne,* picturesquely sited at Champillon near Ay, *Berceaux* at Epernay and *Cheval Blanc* at Sept Sauls have one: the *Restaurant de la Gare* at Epernay, too, still has its nostalgically faithful friends.

The landscape is not spectacular, but it is pleasing and, with familiarity, beguiling. Often it recalls the English Downland. In many places hills of this height – less than 280 metres above sea level and only about 180 from the surrounding plain – would be unremarkable, but in such flat country they are impressive, dominant, stimulating; they give character to the countryside. Below them the

Marne follows a reluctant, twisting, yet stately course and the N3, the Marne-Rhine canal and the railway join its east-west line in near-parallel. This countryside is quiet, softly rounded, for the sharp edges of the hills' violent birth have been weathered smooth: yet, looking down from the Mountain of Reims or Hautvillers to the Marne, the scene is unforgettably rich. The glory of this country lies in its vines; not merely for their wine – which is supreme – but for the sight of them, like a vast, serried green army – their lines set at different angles to distinguish one grower's strip from another's: and, as the *vendange* approaches, heavy, thickset with their crop. The villages are widely spaced, for it is not the fashion of the peasant grower to waste good vineyard land on buildings. When they do appear, the church spire flourished like a pennant over the sea of vines, they are modest, drably coloured, inward-looking – showing few windows – yet at one with their surroundings. Most of the villagers work in the vines or in the cellars of Reims or Epernay and, at the *vendange,* there is hardly a lane, alley or courtyard of the village where pressing is not in progress, identified by a thin trickle of grape-juice running into the street or under a wooden gate. Then the vineyards are full of pickers, the roads of every kind of vehicle bringing the fruit down to the presses and brokers, *manipulants,* technicians, tourists and the local tradesmen are all involved in the comings and goings of this crown of the wine-year.

One important aspect of the Champagne region and more significantly of the wine territory is not immediately apparent. The cellars of Champagne are unique; some of them were described in the last century as 'wonders of the world' and they still attract some thousands of visitors today. They are cut out of the chalk and they play a crucial part in the making of champagne because it is essential that sparkling wine is matured over a substantial period at an extremely low and consistent temperature. These cellars remain at a steady 12° centigrade – 10° at the lowest level – even in the hottest weather. Because the ageing process must take place in bottle, the champagne-makers need relatively more cellar space than other *vignerons*.

The chalk works easily and the *Champenois* have become expert in tunnelling it. In many cases the workmen simply sank a shaft on the shipper's land and then, like coal-miners, dug galleries and corridors at different levels;

though these are much wider and higher than those of coal mines. Some of the bigger cellars have two or even three tiers of galleries, all piped and wired for water, drainage, ventilation and electric lighting. Many of them are so large that formerly horses and carts were used as they might have been in the streets above; bicycles are normal and, in modern times, not only fork trucks, but cars are used in the frequent removal of bottles and men.

The most remarkable cellarage is that of the Butte Saint Nicaise now occupied by the shippers Ruinart Père et Fils, Charles Heidsieck and, most spectacularly, by Pommery et Greno where the different architectural styles, wall carvings and a vast staircase create a place of fantasy. These were originally quarries worked by the Romans to provide chalk building blocks. To protect the workings against rain or frost which would impair the quality of the chalk, they were not worked in opencast fashion. Instead, the diggers – presumably slaves – made their way in at ground level through a hole small enough to be covered against the weather. Then they proceeded to dig downwards and outwards until finally they had made a huge pyramid-shaped excavation. Since these diggings were connected by tunnels and had stairs by which the slaves could make their way to and from the surface, they serve admirably as wine cellars.

The whole townships of tunnels under Reims, Epernay, Ay and parts of Châlons-sur-Marne are said to extend in all to some 450 kilometres; and to be capable of accommodating more than 200 million bottles of champagne.

This underground showpiece is not simply ideal storage space for wine, but it is an immense tourist attraction giving the shippers admirable value in publicity, public relations and even a captive audience at a 'point of sale'.

Champagne demands more of its makers than most wines. Its production method took longer to develop than any; and, ultimately, it is the most complex of all in terms of production.

In Bordeaux, Burgundy or Alsace a man may produce his own wine in virtual isolation. His vines grow within the walls of his own vineyard; he presses the grapes in the press house attached to his home; matures them in his own *chai*; bottles them there and sends them away without having to step off his own land. The champagne maker is in an altogether different – indeed, almost opposite – situation. In Bordeaux and Burgundy, especially, it is regarded as a major virtue in a wine that it is made from the grapes of a single vineyard only, and authenticated by being made, bottled and labelled on the premises. Champagne, to do itself justice, must be a blended wine, made from different kinds of grapes, from different vineyards in different micro-climates. So, during the nineteenth century, a system developed in which growers and makers were separate – sometimes opposing – groups. Nowadays some growers sell their own champagne as *récoltants-manipulants*. Others have formed powerful and efficient co-operatives which some use only for vinification, others for the entire process to bottling and sale. Meanwhile an increasing number of makers have substantially extended their vineyard holdings. Traditionally, however, the makers travelled the various parts of the *vignoble* inspecting, negotiating, supervising pressings, before they returned to their *celliers* to direct the blending and subsequent processes. The growers, for their part, have always sought to disperse their vine-plots in the attempt to avoid damage from the usually localized, violent summer thunderstorms characteristic of the area. Although their holdings are small (three-quarters of them own less than a hectare – $2\frac{1}{2}$ acres; a third less than half an acre) they often have plots as much as five or six miles apart. So the *vignerons* of champagne have always been mobile. In Bordeaux a *négociant* with an office in Bordeaux might never go to St. Emilion, or vice versa; but in Champagne, although there is rivalry between Reims and Epernay, there is close contact between them. The office of the *Comité Interprofessionel du Vin de Champagne* (CIVC) is in Epernay: but the champagne growers' club is in Reims: and the much-used road between the two passes, straight as a dropped stone, over the Montagne de Reims.

It is important to recognize that champagne as we know it is a modern wine; young by comparison with the historic still wines of Bordeaux and Burgundy. It is little more than a century ago that it first became possible consistently to produce clear, sparkling champagne in safe bottles. Technical changes still go on in its manufacture. There is often reference to the traditions of champagne – and, certainly, under the law it must be vinified 'in accordance with the traditional methods of the region'. Yet it is an industry in flux, the standards which makers regarded, and growers accepted, as established and invariable a hundred years ago become yearly less constant. Its structure contains some inbuilt political, economic and psychological conflicts which do not occur in other winefields. They have been recognized and partly understood for more than sixty years but are no nearer being resolved now than they were then. They involve not only the people of the region but the character, quality and image of the wine itself.

For the visitor to the district the *Comité Interprofessionel du Vin de Champagne* has devised three *Routes de Champagne*: the blue route runs from Reims round the Montagne de Reims to Ay: the red along the Marne Valley and back to Epernay; the green from Epernay through the Côtes des Blancs. They now are the routes of tourism; but the *Champenois* have followed them for centuries. Their new, secondary but important, value lies in leading tourists off the fast roads and into a countryside which grows into the mind through the eyes – green, fresh, uncomplicated, simple, earthy.

Such are the facets of the concept of champagne – *le champagne*, the wine which is an idea and an image; *la Champagne*, the ancient kingdom; *les Champenois*, the people who give it life; and *la Champagne viticole* – the vineyard region.

2

Krug: a facet of champagne

The facets of champagne are reflected in the house of Krug.
Here the word house is used in all four senses – as a
commercial establishment, a store-place, a family through
its generations, and their actual buildings.

The Krug family make – and are deeply involved with –
a *marque* of champagne. They live contentedly in the
province of Champagne. They are *Champenois*; their
ancestor settled there, became one of its people by
language, life-style and official citizenship; and his
descendants bore arms in the French army.

La Champagne viticole has become their natural habitat;
they know the folds of its land, the shape and lines of its
crops; the faces, the families, the houses, the grapes and the
pressed juices of the growers. They in their turn are
known throughout the wine country of Champagne.
When Henri Krug goes out into the vineyards at the
vendange to supervise a grower's pressing, he often is
renewing a relationship that has existed for five generations.

The Krug family tree, as related to the champagne house

(Johann) Joseph KRUG I
1800–1866
*(Business and control
1843–1866)*

Emma Anne JAUNAY
1810–1879

Paul KRUG I
1842–1910
(Business 1860–1910)
(Control 1866–1910)

Caroline HARLÉ
1846–1915

(10 children)

*Joseph (Samuel) KRUG II
1869–1967
(Business 1893–1965)
(Control 1910–1959)

Jeanne HOLLIER-LAROUSSE
1880–1954
(Business 1915–1918)

Paul (Jacques) KRUG II
1912–
(Business 1934–   )
(Control 1941–   )

Jacqueline FORT
1911–

(5 children)

Henri KRUG—Odile BURKARD
1937–
(Business 1965–   )
(General Manager 1970–   )

Rémi KRUG—Catherine BOUTIN
1942–
(Business 1968–   )
(General Manager 1970–   )

(3 children)

(3 children)

*From 1926–1941 Joseph Krug II controlled the Company with his cousin, Jean Seydoux, and in 1941 Paul Krug II joined them. Joseph Krug II retired in 1959 leaving the control of the Company in the hands of Paul Krug II and Jean Seydoux. This partnership continued until 1962 when Jean Seydoux died. Paul Krug II continued in sole control of the Company until 1970 when his sons, Henri and Rémi, were appointed general managers with their father and, at the same time, Rémi was elected to the Board.

Krug is but one of the 144 houses making champagne. It is the theme of this book because it is outstanding – indeed, unique. Cyril Ray, in his monograph on Bollinger, observed 'Almost – not quite but almost – invariably, if I asked the maker or agent of one of the great champagnes what wine he would drink if he did not drink his own, the answer would be either Krug or Bollinger or, often enough, both – bracketed equal, or as alternatives to each other, or either one first with the other a close second.'

Patrick Forbes who, in his deep and wide study *Champagne,* deals with the subject in all its aspects more perceptively and thoroughly than any Englishman – or, probably, any Frenchman – has ever done, describes Krug there as 'a very small firm with a world-wide reputation for producing the very best champagne.'

No author, however, undertakes the writing of a book because of other people's superlatives. The choice is generally dictated – as in this case – by the subject itself.

Apart from a privileged minority, the English generally know less about champagne than about other wines. That applies to many who are enthusiastic – and even informed – students of wine in general. That is not to say they have never tasted it, but that their range of experience is too limited to be critical. The first reason for that fact is economic. Champagne is dear. It can only rarely and expensively be bought by the glass. It is not possible – as it is with burgundy or claret – for the novice to begin with a genuinely cheap bottle and work up the scale of quality to a thoroughly sound one, like for instance, an honest, *bourgeois château* claret which is still within reach of the average pocket. The truth is that few people drink champagne regularly; it has no *'ordinaire'*; it is the wine of occasion. The Englishman's nonconformist conscience, too, has restricted him: although he no longer accepts the Victorian concept of champagne as the villain's lure to trap the innocent maiden, there still remains an element of disapproval on the grounds that it is 'extravagant'.

The most powerful influence of all, however, is simple lack of knowledge. When most of us drink it – generally at a wedding or christening – the host is not a wealthy man. Often on the advice of the caterer he may decide that one of the cheaper brands – what the makers call 'wedding champagne' and sometimes even labelled for coronations and other open air festivities – is adequate for a mass, uncritical and probably bibulous company. It is likely then to be drunk in an atmosphere more conducive to gaiety than critical judgement: so assessment of the wine is based solely on the thick head of the following morning. It is, too, the fact that cheap champagne is extremely poor: so much poorer than the best as to be almost a different drink. Thus many British people who have drunk some dozens of bottles of champagne in the course of their lives without ever tasting a good one, tend to think of it as a stimulating drink but not a 'serious' wine. Certainly that was true of this writer.

For him that heresy was dispelled in Reims in 1973. The champagne was Krug 1966; drunk in the company of the family it had to be taken seriously. Colour good; nose rich and full, even a little austere; the flavour was simply a fresh experience to one who had never known the 'taste of Krug'. The enduring dilemma of the wine-writer is the lack of precise language to define and communicate the

bouquet and flavour of a wine to a reader. There are many technical terms, but they are professional in-talk and do not convey a clear impression to the ordinary drinker. Thus while someone finding a wine tart might call it 'acid', that, to a wine taster, means an adequate proportion of the desirable – indeed, essential – ingredient (a combination of hydracids and oxyacids) which gives it its freshness and bite. Liken the taste to that of apples and the expert understands a raw and immature – 'green' – wine. In full consciousness of these limitations – the scent of that first glass of Krug was rich and flowery; the flavour clean, clear and utterly distinct; strong and deep, yet elegant; it had what the tasters call 'finesse' – or 'breeding'. It had, in short, the unique 'taste of Krug': and, despite the (hindsight) complexity of its blending, it was a complete unity. It was unquestionably a great white wine, entitled to as much respect as the most eminent *crus* of the Côte d'Or.

Conversion from indifference by way of repentance to enthusiasm was – like most conversions – rapid. The impression was reinforced by subsequent – rare, but impressive – tastings. It may be possible to become satiated with Krug champagne; it is said that Mr Nubar Gulbenkian did: but our bank balances preserve the rest of us from that macabre fate.

Krug is a fine and a rare champagne. For a commodity of its quality it has been modestly handled. Perhaps it would be truer to say that only a commodity of such quality could be handled so modestly. It makes no attempt to catch the eye. It is never 'packaged' more elaborately than in a wooden box, with the name branded on the end, for a presentation magnum. The foil, in avoiding the possible garishness of gilt, is bronze in colour; the shoulder label (*collerette*) a sombrely deep purple; the label severe black-on-white name and a crest. No one has ever seen an advertisement for Krug. Nowhere in Champagne will you see that name – as you do those of other *marques* – painted on the sides of houses, on hoardings, on vineyard walls, on vehicles. In the whole region the name is displayed in only one place – on the small engraved brass plate on the wall of the head office at 5 Rue Coquebert in Reims.

Its reputation depends solely – and loftily – on the recommendation of those who know it; and, for the greater proportion of its sales, on those who are accustomed to the distinctive Krug flavour and have no wish to drink any other.

Since the foundation of the house in 1843 it has come down in direct line of descent through the eldest sons. It is one wine; it has no *sous marques,* no 'luxury' version; it is simply the best champagne the house of Krug can make. That, by expert consent, is the finest champagne in the world. It is certainly the dearest.

Champagne is, above all others, a 'made' wine, depending entirely upon the skill of its maker. Krug champagne has always been made, personally, through detailed selection, blending decisions and supervision, by the senior member – except in unavoidable circumstances the eldest male – of the Krug family.

It is an exclusive wine. In recent years it has been rationed even to long-established customers; but it is exclusive chiefly by virtue of its price. It is expensive because it employs, unstintingly, the most expensive commodity in the world today – labour. It has been expertly estimated that, from vine to drinker, a bottle of Krug champagne is handled almost three hundred times. It is not possible to understand champagne – or why it costs as much as it does – without understanding how it is made.

3

The making of champagne

The process of making champagne is legally defined and named. It is the making of sparkling wine through a secondary fermentation in bottle; and it is known as the *méthode champenoise*. That process may be – and is – carried out beyond the boundaries of *la Champagne viticole*: but the end-product may not by French law, take the name of champagne. True champagne is made by that process from specified types of grapes, grown and pruned according to local regulations in defined vineyard areas in Marne, Haute Marne, Aisne and Aube; and vinified there in accordance with the traditional practice of the country. Some grapes which are entitled to the *appellation* are sold to makers of sparkling wines in other districts: but their product may not be called champagne. Even the original still red and white wines of the region, made there since the earliest days, are not entitled to the name champagne but must be called *Coteaux Champenois*. They are now only a small proportion of the whole production: notably a Blanc de Blancs, a full white wine made by several houses but not widely exported; and the historic Bouzy rouge, once the favourite of kings.

Champagne is not a natural wine; quite the reverse. Still wine is a natural process. Throw some grapes into a container and the juice that runs out of them will ferment to produce a liquid which, in chemical terms, is wine. The best still wines are made by controlled use of that natural process. Champagne, however, is a far more sophisticated creation and, for that reason, it is not known, like other wines, by the name of its place of origin, but by the *'marque'* of its maker, who is often called a shipper.

Particular skill is called for in the first place even to produce an adequate crop of wine-grapes in Champagne. It is the most northerly vineyard area of France; subject to spring frosts which can wipe out a crop even in May. Hybrids might throw a second bloom after such damage; but no hybrids – only 'noble grapes' – may be grown in the region.

Normally heavy summer rains and occasional utterly destructive hail storms add to the problems of the growers and, although the *Champenois* declare optimistically that they invariably enjoy an 'Indian summer' for the *vendange,* it rained every day for three weeks at the picking of 1974. The forest on the plateau of the Mountain of Reims provides shelter and regulated humidity for vines set not too high on the slope but high enough to escape all except the sharpest frosts. The mean temperature is, by the narrowest margin, adequate for the cultivation of wine grapes.

Nevertheless before sparkling champagne was made, the still wines – grey or pink but lacking in colour and tart in taste – seem to have been regarded as inferior to those of the sunnier climate of Burgundy.

Although some other species are permitted by law, the grapes of Champagne are effectively the *pinot noir* and the *chardonnay*, the *cépages* (grape-types) used for the fine red and white wines of Burgundy, and the best champagne is made from a mixture of the two. The law allows the use of *pinot meunier*, a late-blooming, early-ripening vine which gives a second quality wine; *arbanne* (a little is grown near Bar-sur-Arbe) and the *petit meslier*, a delicately flavoured white grape but highly vulnerable to blight. The *chardonnay* is sometimes called *pinot blanc* but it is not a true *pinot*: in fact, a genuine white-bearing *pinot* does exist, though it is dying out in both Champagne and Burgundy. *Chardonnay* is the white grape of the Côtes des Blancs which contributes scent, delicacy – and a quarter of the volume – to champagne. The noble *pinot noir* – in several variants, including the *gros plant doré d'Ay* – provides, with its golden juice, the body and power and 60 per cent of the bulk of the wine. Although the *pinot noir* is a black grape, its juice is white so long as the skins are removed from the *must* (unfermented juice) before the pigment emerges. In fact a full-bodied Blancs de Noirs is sometimes made from them; while a Blanc de Blancs from the *chardonnay* is notably light and delicate.

The best grapes come from the communes within the Marne *département*; the black grape *crus* of the sickle-shaped area of the Mountain of Reims (generally divided into *vins de la Montagne* and *vins de la rivière*): and the whites of the Côtes des Blancs, south of the river in a roughly similar formation below Epernay. Importantly, too, virtually all the officially approved vineyard land in Marne is already under vines; so any further planting can take place only in less suitable parts of the region. The best grapes are in increasingly short supply, a situation which could cause difficulties, differences and shifts of economic emphasis in the early future.

A few days before the grapes are ready to be picked, a commission of the CIVC formed of makers and growers – with a government commissioner to hold the balance – agrees and announces the price to be paid for the crop. *'Prix du raisin'* appears as a table of some two hundred growths – with all-over figures for the outlying vineyards of Dormans; of the Aube; the *'crus non cotés'* of the Marne; and most of those of Aisne. Certain outstanding vineyards – eleven in 1973 – are awarded a figure of 100 per cent and they are paid the full *'prix de base'*. The remainder are scaled down, in proportion to merit, formerly to 50 per cent, but now only to 77 per cent (for the distant communes of Aube and Aisne) of the agreed maximum figure.

The 100 per cent *crus* are Ambonnay, Beaumont-sur-Vesle, Bouzy, Louvois, Mailly, Sillery and Verzenay of the black *montagne* grapes; Ay of the *rivière*; Avize and Cramant from the *chardonnay* vineyards of the Côte des Blancs. They, of course, sell their grapes easily, but other, and lesser, growers used often to have difficulty in doing so. The present arrangements give them a guarantee that their entire crop will be taken – regardless of quality – unless they choose to go into the open market.

The nineteenth-century shape of the champagne industry was, almost inevitably for a blended product, one of separate operations by growers on one hand, makers on the other. That line of demarcation, however, has become increasingly blurred in this century. Since 1945, *récoltants-manipulants* sales show an increase from $1\frac{1}{2}$ million to 35 million bottles. Of the 1973 champagne grape harvest, half was 'engaged' – contracted for by the makers who were bound to accept it – one third was used by *récoltants-manipulants*; and one sixth went onto the free market.

The co-operatives are active at all stages; in some cases vinifying grapes for growers who then bottle and sell it themselves; in others, carrying out the entire process through to labelling, either for an individual grower or in the name of the co-operative.

During the inter-War depression a number of makers refused to pay the growers' asking price for the fine – now unquestionably 100 per cent – grapes of Mailly. The local growers, despite their scanty resources, set up a co-operative – putting up the building with their own hands – and now make and bottle their own vintage and non-vintage champagne. A number of other communes followed their example in varying degrees. Thus the growers have, to a considerable extent, released the resentment and achieved the security, bargaining power and emancipation which provided the basic motivation for the Ay riots. The financial – above all, by inescapable inference, class – barrier which existed in the nineteenth century between growers and houses has thus been assailed, if not destroyed. Meanwhile, shippers are no longer free to choose the grapes most suitable for their purpose but, in some cases, must accept an allocation they do not want. The new – *touristique* – *Route de Champagne* has proved a considerable sales-aid to the growers. Tourists find it attractive to stop at a vineyard, taste and buy the grower's own champagne and, in many cases, arrange for a subsequent supply bearing his label which, because it is little known, seems, for that reason, personal to them. On the other hand, the established houses still control the major proportion of the export trade. Even at the *vendange* the interests of the two groups are not identical, as they were in the period of free bargaining. Some makers think that the guarantees of price and complete purchase have caused many growers to put quantity before quality; growers tend to think the opposite of the makers. Eventually, however, the reputation and the sales of champagne must depend on quality.

The date for the picking to start is given by the *Préfet* – on the decision of the CIVC in an *Ouverture des Vendanges*. It is usually in September: exceptionally in August; hazardously, when the grapes have been slow to ripen, in October. Then the vast army of *vendangeurs* – mostly from the industrial areas of northern France – moves in and picking goes on, uninterrupted and at the

highest possible speed, for fear of rain, with its attendant danger of rot.

Under-ripe grapes in Champagne particularly are likely to be crucially deficient in sugar: if over-ripe, they lack acid and, in the case of the red, the pigment is likely to colour the juice. If a vintage is of doubtful or mixed quality, a maker may insist on *épluchage,* the expensive process of picking out rotten grapes by hand. Perfection is hard to achieve: but once the harvest – good or bad – is gathered, all that follows is in the hands of experts.

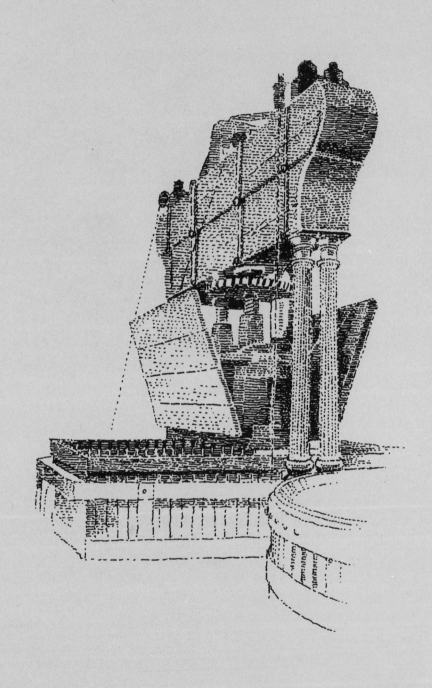

The pressing is supervised by the buyer of grapes; members of the Krug family may be at a dozen press houses in the course of a single day during the *vendange*. The traditional champagne press – called a *maie* – is made of oak; it holds 4,000 kilogrammes of grapes, is set close to the ground and designed to press firmly, but not hard enough to drive the colour of the red grape skins into the juice. There are three pressings; 2,000 litres of the first '*serre*' are called the *vin de cuvée*; the next two – each of 666 litres – also entitled to the *appellation* – are the *première* and *deuxieme tailles*: finally, the last dregs of juice – not permitted to be used for champagne – are called the *rebèche*.

The *must* is stabilized and cleansed by the addition of a little sulphur, piped or transported to the *négoçiant's* cellars and, if necessary, chaptalized – dosed with sugar to improve its alcohol content – and left to ferment, usually, nowadays, in glass or steel-lined vats.

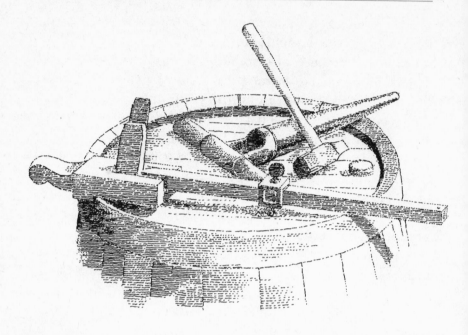

Of old this first fermentation always took place in oak casks, as it still does at Bollinger and Krug.

The process of fermentation is impressive, even alarming : for a week or more the *must* is almost volcanic in its heavings. It settles, is racked of its impurities and left, the output of each vineyard still kept separate, until the blending plan is devised. Sometimes a *vin de cru* is made from the *finage* of one vineyard, but no single growth approaches the potential of a well-made blend.

This is the crucial phase in the making of champagne : it decides the entire character of the *cuvée*. The most expert blender cannot produce a great result from poor wines: but he will make the most of his materials. Only an outstanding blender working with fine – and correctly chosen – ingredients can create a great champagne. He works in an almost sterile room, free from any intrusive odour, for he must not only judge the *cuvées* as they are, but foresee and assess what they will be after blending, secondary fermentation and maturing; testing, making trial tastings, selecting, rejecting; looking ahead through all the changes these raw, sharp wines will undergo on their way to being drunk. Again, this process formerly was undertaken by the head of the firm; that happens now only rarely: in most houses it is done by the cellar-master or the firm's chemists.

Although the grapes are grown in Champagne and are limited to two species, the gradations of difference between the belemite and micaster chalk, the variations in micro-climate and aspect between vineyards produce wines of widely varying character. The wines of the Montagne are the most alcoholic: well rounded with plenty of body, yet never heavy. All the *pinot noir* wines have delicate taste and marked bouquet. The Mareuil vineyards are known for body and vinosity; those from Ludes and Chigny les Roses for body; Rilly appreciably lighter; Sillery and Verzenay are rich in bouquet; Ambonnay, Bouzy and Louvois, outstanding for body and balance; those of Ay for their finesse, and the combination of liveliness and fullness.

On the other side of the river, the *chardonnay* of the Côte des Blancs give delicate, fresh, elegant, slow-maturing wines; those of Avize are pale in colour and light in character; of Cramant, bigger and more scented; of le Mesnil-sur-Oger fresh, often *pétillant*; of Grauves notably clean with a 'gun-flint' flavour. These characteristics, their capacity for blending and development with age, must be in the blender's memory and his forward look.

A demonstration of this skill by Paul Krug was an amazing revelation. He put out for tasting glasses of eight different young wines which had not undergone their second fermentation. Then he mixed numbers one and two; three and four; five and six; seven and eight; in different proportions. Tasting showed that the two-wine blends had taken on fresh flavours. He poured the first of the blends into the second; the third into the fourth: again they had assumed new characters. Finally he blended those two mixtures in proportions of three to two; the result was a wine of depth and quality never to be perceived in the eight original glasses. This was for him an elementary exercise. In 1969 he composed a *Brut Réserve* from forty-nine different *crus*.

The decreed blending is carried out by the cellar-master. Then the wine is given about twenty-three grammes to the litre of the *liqueur de tirage* – sugar-cane, yeasts, tannin and fining – to clear it and ensure its development, and put into bottles which are stacked horizontally in the cellars. Duly, as the sap rises in the vines outside for the next harvest, the secondary fermentation takes place in the lately-bottled wine. The subsequent process of champanization is both historic and personalized. The cellars of Champagne are a crucial factor in the making of the wine. Essentially they retain a steady, low temperature of 10°–12° centigrade all the year round, perfect conditions for storing wine.

Legally, non-vintage champagne must mature for a year in bottle, and vintage for three years from the date of picking, before it can be sold. In practice the better houses leave it in their cellars for two to three years, or three to five years, respectively, before they sell it.

Dom Pierre Pérignon is not the patron saint of champagne only because he was never canonized. From

1668 to 1715 he was cellar-master of the Benedictine abbey of Hautvillers, handsomely sited halfway up the southern slope of the Montagne de Reims, looking down across the Marne towards Epernay. The views, both to and from its site, across the vines, are among the most picturesque in Champagne. The abbey church and the cloisters remain. The church stands out handsomely: its stone walls light grey, the turret-dome, dark grey, trees a solid mass of dark green above it; its vineyards running away over the rounded hillocks below, and the entire foreground a vast army of vines. On the foothills of the Montagne with varied crops of maize and sugar beet, the pace of fall is suddenly arrested and all gives way to pasture in gentle country where the clay pockets hold more water than good wine grapes need. Dom Pérignon was a scholarly and highly accomplished maker of champagne, certainly one of the first to blend it successfully. In his later days he lost his sight, but in his blindness his perception of taste became amazingly sharp. It used to be related – perhaps apocryphally but indicative of the respect for his skill – that by tasting a grape he could identify not only the vineyard it came from, but which part of the vineyard.

It has been extravagantly claimed for him that he 'put the bubbles into champagne'. He made no such claim and, in fact, it cannot be so: its northerly climate ensures that wine made in Champagne will undergo a secondary fermentation; or, to be more accurate, complete its fermentation in two phases. When that process took place in barrel, the carbon dioxide simply escaped and the end-product was a still wine. André Simon has adduced evidence to argue that, in 1665, the fifth Duke of Bedford's steward bought the bottles and corks for a barrel of young champagne. Contemporary references indicate that the English knew sparkling wine before Dom Pérignon took up his post at Hautvillers. Patrick Forbes, too, argues perceptively that strong, English-made bottles and Spanish corks (to replace the rag plugs of previous general use) were available in England to imprison the secondary fermentation of fresh champagne imported there in barrel. He deduces, though, that, once these facilities became available to Dom Pérignon, he carried out the sequence of blending, bottling, corking and cellaring champagne of good quality, through secondary fermentation, to sparkling maturity. He must surely have been the first man to perform that full process. His wine, however, was misty with impurities and sediments, and erratic – frequently explosive – in gas content.

Whatever may be the truth as to Dom Pérignon's contribution to the development of champagne, there is no doubt that the problem of sediment was solved by *la Veuve* Clicquot. The daughter of a Reims clothmaker, she married, at twenty, the twenty-three year old son of a champagne-maker of the city. Eight years afterwards, soon after their first child – a daughter – was born, her husband died of a fever. She determined to carry on his wine business in Reims – an extremely unusual and unconventional course for a young widow in the France of 1806. She took risks, especially in sending her representatives and goods into the export markets of a Europe torn by the Napoleonic Wars. She herself concentrated on the cellar-offices in Reims and her vineyards at Oger: the business flourished.

Her travellers, however, reported complaints from customers about cloudy champagne, whose thick froth resembled toad's eyes. The general solution then was to filter – when all the sparkle was lost – or to decant, with almost as dispiriting effect, and at immense cost in time and labour. The widow Clicquot applied herself to the problem. Eventually she evolved the practice of shaking the bottles and up-ending them into holes cut in long narrow tables until the sediment settled near the cork. It was then possible to extract the cork, with the sediment, and re-cork, preserving the crucial sparkle. Gradually she evolved the method – resolved by 1816 – of tilting the tables (*pupîtres*) and cutting elliptical holes in them to take the bottles, by the neck, at first nearly horizontally, then, in the fashion which is still used, of *remuage*, each bottle was given a series of one-eighth turns towards a slightly steeper angle. An experienced *remueur* can 'riddle' 32,000 bottles a day. After three complete revolutions – twenty-four shakings – the bottle should be *sur pointe* – vertical – and the sediment will have settled on the cork. Then the cork is removed – with the sediment – the bottle topped up and recorked with the 'sparkle' still imprisoned.

The remaining problem was solved by the man who is now accepted as the third immortal of champagne, though at the time no one so much as noted his Christian name. Bottles still exploded under the pressure of the carbonic acid gas to a degree both costly and dangerous. As late as 1816 it was estimated that, in different cellars, anything from 15 per cent to 40 per cent of the stock was lost by bursting: Vizetelly in his *Facts About Champagne* put the figure as high as 60 per cent. In 1836 a chemist from

Châlons-sur-Marne, recalled simply as M. François, published a paper on some experiments he had conducted. They consisted of measuring the amount of unfermented sugar in a wine and, thence, calculating how much carbonic acid gas would be generated by subsequent fermentation. Thus, for the first time, the maker had some ascertainable guidance on how much sugar he ought to include in his *liqueur de tirage* in order to ensure sparkle while avoiding explosion. At once the number of bursting bottles fell to about 10 per cent. Even at that figure a cellar

could be a perilous place during the period of the secondary fermentation and the workers there still retained their iron masks as protection against the flying glass. The immense advances in the quality of glass 'metal' and the making of bottles provided a steadily increasing measure of safety. At length, early in this century, an Epernay research chemist, H E Manceau – who also played a considerable part in the local counter-measures against the plague of phylloxera – discovered an even more precise method than François' of measuring the sugar content. As a result, breakages now do not amount to one per cent. That represents a considerable achievement by comparison with the state of affairs described by one nineteenth-century observer who reported that 120,000 out of 200,000 bottles were destroyed in the cellars of a single well-known firm. The fact remains, however, that a champagne bottle – or for that matter, any sparkling wine bottle – can be lethal; the pressure inside it is the same as that inside the tyre of a London bus.

Dégorgement – the final part of the Veuve Clicquot's process for clearing the wine was originally an even more highly skilled operation than it is now. The *dégorgeur* took off the cramp, held the bottle downwards to keep the sediment on the base of the first cork which he removed with a twist, as he turned the bottle almost upright. The release of gas blew out the sediment, but a good *dégorgeur* prevented any appreciable escape of the sparkle while the loss of volume was made good by the addition of the appropriate amount of cane sugar to produce the degree of sweetness the market for that bottle demanded. Up to $1\frac{1}{2}$ per cent produces *brut* (or *nature*); $1\frac{1}{2}$ per cent to 2 per cent, *extra sec*; 2 per cent to 4 per cent, *sec* (or *gout Americain*); 4 per cent to 6 per cent *demi-sec* (or *gout Français*); and 8 per cent to 10 per cent *doux*. While, in theory, a true *brut* would

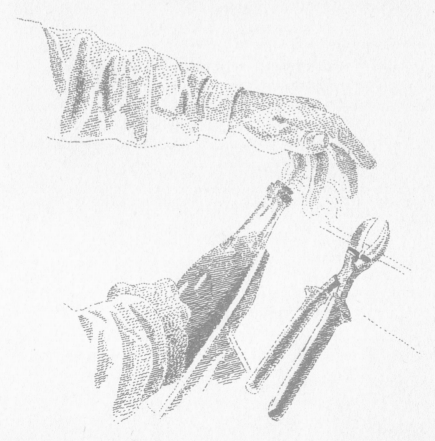

have no added sugar at all, it is extremely rare in practice for any house not to add a small quantity. The 8 per cent to 10 per cent for *doux* is quite unusual nowadays, except sometimes for the South American market: the normal maximum is 4 per cent, though during the last century Russia demanded as much as 16 per cent. The wine-sugar solution used for the dosage is called the *liqueur d'expédition*. The *dégorgeur*'s final task – and all must be done with speed to retain the carbonic acid gas – is to examine the wine by eye against the light to ensure that no sediment remains and, by smelling, to check that it is pure and uncontaminated. His task has been made simpler in recent years by passing the bottle, neck foremost, through refrigerating fluid before it reaches him, so that the sediment will come out in a blob of ice frozen to the cork. The chilling also has the effect of reducing the pressure. Nowadays – again to the end of retaining the gas – almost all makers add the *liqueur d'expédition* by conducting it to the bottling installation through silver pipes to avoid possible contamination by other metals.

Then the bottle passes to the *boucheur* to be given its final cork. This is a surprisingly bulky-looking piece of cork – which must by law carry the word 'Champagne' on the

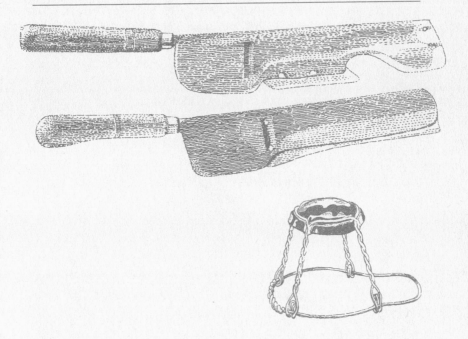

side, and generally has the maker's name on the base. It is squeezed by the corking machine to half its size and a huge power-driven hammer is used to force it so far into the neck of the bottle that the bottom begins to spread – which gives it added grip against the possibility of being blown out. It is secured by the little net of wire which is prevented by a metal disc from cutting into the cork. Then each bottle is checked – once more for clarity and to ascertain that it is full measure – and shaken to mix in the dosage. Finally it is given the elaborate trappings traditional for all sparkling wines, but particularly champagne. A foil cap has replaced the wax originally used to conceal loss during the *dégorgement* when it was so excessive that to make it good with the *liqueur d'expédition* would have resulted in an unacceptably sweet bottle. Now it hides the slightly unsightly bulging cork, wire and disc. Neck label and main label are stuck on.

Almost all these processes – quite a proliferation by comparison with those required for still wine – involve, of course, a vast amount of labour. That commodity was cheap in the early days of the fashion for champagne; now it is expensive; so, too, are the experience and skills required in the more expert operations. Almost all the work, though, can be simulated, accelerated or facilitated by machinery or chemicals. It is a matter for individual shippers to decide what effect those aids are likely to have on the end product, and the extent to which they will employ them.

Many have found themselves forced to take short cuts by the competition less from other champagne shippers than from other sparkling wines.

These are now made in almost all wine-producing countries; many of them most capably – especially those for which the *méthode champenoise* is used. There are two other processes for making sparkling wine, the Charmat (or *cuve close*), and simple carbonisation. The Charmat process, originated by the French wine-chemist Eugène Charmat, consists of pumping the wine through a series of vats in which it is 'aged' by heating, cooled, fermented by the addition of yeasts and sugar, clarified and filtered in closed tanks so that the gas cannot escape. Carbonisation is simply the process used by the aerated drinks manufacturers in which carbon dioxide is pumped into the wine.

Those made by the *méthode champenoise* are the best, though the Charmat process has its merits; the carbonated

wines, however, are poor. Virtually every region of France makes a sparkling wine, most of them by the champagne process. Nothing, though, can ever truly simulate a genuine fine champagne produced from a blend of the red and white grapes grown on that rare chalk soil and matured in those deep, cold, chalk cellars. The French law which forbids a wine from any other region being called champagne is not merely a matter of guarding a vested interest. The wine of Champagne, despite all the processes it undergoes, is sparkling by nature because, in the course of its life in that particular climate, without prompting or contrivance, it undergoes the secondary fermentation which causes it to sparkle. The special operations, which are not necessary in the case of still wines, are designed simply to preserve the sparkle of that secondary fermentation and to clear the wine. Other regions can, and do, make successful still wines for which they use their best grapes. Therefore – and Burgundy is a strong case in point – they tend to make a sparkling wine from their lesser grapes. That, too, explains the fact that they are often rather sweet. It is true of some lesser *cuvées* of champagne as well, for sugar will hide deficiencies and flaws in a sparkling – or any other – wine which would be exposed beyond all question if the wine remained dry.

Other sparkling wines of France made by the *méthode champenoise* are often palatable and refreshing, but they may describe themselves only as '*mousseux*' – not champagne. That point was upheld in England – though under a completely different aspect of the law – in 1960. Two years earlier a prosecution by the *Comité Interprofessionel du Vin de Champagne* and the British Association of Champagne Importers brought a case in the Central Criminal Court – under the Merchandise Marks Act – against a British firm of wine importers who had sold a sparkling wine as 'Spanish Champagne'. The defence adduced such similarly misleading labels as 'Spanish Sauternes', 'British Tarrogna', 'Chilean Barsac' and 'Australian Burgundy'. The case was lost and the 'pure' champagne plaintiffs were ordered to pay the – extremely heavy – costs. The decision caused something of a diplomatic crisis between France and Britain and questions were asked in Parliament. Soon afterwards, however, the twelve *grande marque* champagne houses – who include Krug – boldly, and at risk of still higher costs than in the previous case, combined to bring an action against the same firm in the Chancery Division of the High Court for the offence of 'passing off'. Before the trial of that matter could begin there was a preliminary hearing – which lasted a week – to decide whether the shippers themselves had the right to the name. It was held that they had; the case was opened and, at length, in a delayed judgment, Mr Justice Danckwerts found for the shippers, forbade the use of the word 'champagne' on the label of the Spanish wine, and granted costs to the plaintiffs. As the consequence of his decision, he prevented any and every sparkling wine made anywhere in the world being sold in England as 'champagne'.

Gradually the rest of the wine-trading world – except the United States of America – conformed to that ruling. The word 'Champagne' on a bottle can now be accepted, almost everywhere, as indicating that it contains the sparkling wine of Champagne. The strong French wine-laws ensure that it conforms to strict regulations governing the prescribed grapes, growing areas, production controls, vinification and maturation. In 1974, too, an English court ruled that cider makers were not entitled to use the word champagne as in 'champagne cider' or 'champagne perry' on their labels.

For 132 years and five generations, the Krug family, in a parallel story, has jealously maintained and defended these involved and expert processes.

4

Joseph Krug I:
Mainz to Reims

The essential history of the house of Krug is that it was founded – somewhat surprisingly but determinedly – by the first Joseph, and continued, with marked devotion, by the eldest sons of his line for five generations.

There were occasions, during the war-service, absence as a prisoner of war, and subsequent illness of Joseph II, and immaturity of Paul II, when the major responsibility was delegated. Otherwise it was zealously embraced by men who maintained a deep devotion to the concept of family – and a family wine.

Filial devotion is by no means always sufficient to sustain a single-minded business under French law, by which an inheritance must be divided between all the children. Indeed, the continuity of the champagne house of Krug owes much to the fact that both the first and second Josephs each had only one child, and that both these children were sons. It survived the fact that Paul I had ten children; and should do so, too, through the division of Paul II's interest between five.

In any family it is unusual to find a direct line of male succession through five generations; in the case of the Krug family in France it is already six. The founder of the Krug family in Reims – Joseph – came from Mainz, a free city when he was born there in 1800.

There is no evidence to show that Johann Joseph Krug grew up with any special knowledge of wine. His father and grandfather were apparently fairly prosperous butchers in Mainz. The vineyards and wines of that city were few and of no great distinction. On the other hand, Mainz was an important clearing house not only for the wines of nearby Rhinehessen but for all those of the Rhine. Formerly a free city, about the time of the birth of J J Krug it constantly changed hands. Ceded to France in 1797 and 1801, it was restored to Germany in 1814, and in 1816 passed into the administration of Rheinhessia.

Life there must have been uncertain enough for the observer not to be surprised that J J Krug looked and moved further afield than the place of his birth.

The first clear surviving picture of him is in a travel permit issued by the Grand Duchy of Hessen for Joseph Krug (he had already dropped the 'Johann', which was also his father's first name) 'trader and commercial traveller' to go to Hanau, sixty kilometres away, on the edge of Frankfurt.

The document shows that at twenty-four he was, by modern standards, short – only five feet two inches (1.57 metres) – with brown eyes, eyebrows and hair; his beard was black, his chin oval, and his complexion healthy. The form cannot express – and was not required to do so – the character apparent in the man's appearance. That is clear in

Monsieur J. Krug, 8 Rue Gros Chenet à Paris

(Châlons s/M) — 20 Novembre 1834

Nous voyons, Monsieur, par votre lettre du 16 ct., que vous êtes disponible et que vous pouvez vous rendre ici à l'époque que nous désirons. L'intérêt de Mr. Friès étant de partir quand vous serez arrivé, veuillez venir le plutôt possible, pour ne pas le retenir plus long tems qu'il ne le désire.

Quant aux appointements, nous vous accordons les mêmes que ceux que nous allouons à Mr. Friès, Frs 2000 — par an; persuadés d'après les renseignements avantageux que nous a donné notre ami Daumer, que vous êtes capable de remplacer Mr. Friès, auquel nous avons accordé ces conditions, parceque nous le connaissions depuis long tems et très capable. Nous laissons à Mr. Floss de vous instruire de ce que vous aurez à faire dans notre maison.

Nous avons l'honneur de vous saluer

Jacquesson f. G.

Joseph Krug I

a rather later – but obviously faithful – portrait now in his great-grandson's house at Reims. This was, beyond all question, a purposeful man. The face strong – with a firm jaw – the eyes are steady, the forehead wide, the mouth full and generous – but sensitive – not that of a ruthless man – one of decision but also, surely, of thought and understanding.

There is no hint of how Joseph Krug spent the next ten years since most of the early family papers were destroyed in the German shelling of their house in Reims during 1915. The next record shows that, in November 1834, he joined the champagne house of Jacquesson et Fils at Châlons-sur-Marne. The letter of engagement lays out the terms in French: his duties are indicated in the final passage, added in German by the German chief clerk: they would consist mainly in attending to shipments, invoicing, making out schedules and cash slips, supervising messengers, and dealing with some correspondence. He was to be paid the same salary as his predecessor – a M. Fries – of 2,000 francs a year. At this time many French commercial houses made a point of engaging German or Swiss clerks – especially for book-keeping – because they found they were generally neater and wrote a better hand than Frenchmen. Certainly this applied in the Krug concern until after the Franco-Prussian war of 1870 when, especially in Champagne, the subsequent occupation caused such bitter feeling against Germans in France.

The firm Joseph Krug had joined was a champagne house of some consequence. Founded by Claude Jacquesson in 1798, it grew rapidly and its establishment near the generous Châlons basin of the Marne-Rhine canal included ten kilometres of cellars wide enough for the passage of horse-drawn wagons, and described, at the beginning of the nineteenth century, as 'one of the wonders of the world'. The firm's reputation was established by a visit from Napoleon in 1810 when he awarded them a gold medal 'for the beauty and splendour of their cellars'. According to the history of the firm, when the Emperor left, his wagons bore a number of cases of their champagne which he drank on the eve of battle; to celebrate his victory over the Austrians at Wagram; at his marriage to Marie-Louise; and at the christening of his son, the King of Rome. For some years the Jacquesson label bore the imperial monogram and a facsimile of the profile of Napoleon which appeared on the star of the Légion d'Honneur. One of their best-known posters showed

Napoleon's Egyptian slave serving his master with *'son champagne préferé'*. A casual yet – for that reason – convincing indication of the extent of their reputation occurs in the Grossmiths' *Diary of a Nobody*, when Mr Pooter, sending the maid round to the grocer for a bottle of Jackson Frères' three-and-sixpenny champagne, suggests that it was something of a nineteenth-century household name, even in England. In 1834 the firm was controlled by the son of the founder, Maurice Jacquesson.

There is no indication of Joseph Krug's reasons for wanting to work in a champagne house, nor of his knowing either the trade or the district. He must himself have sought the recommendation from 'our friend Daumer' – the firm's German agent – which prompted Jacquesson to employ him. He wrote from a lodging in Paris, the house of Monsieur Lebrun – proprietor of an art gallery and husband of Mme Vigée Lebrun, the portrait painter – in the Rue de Gros Chenet, which is now the southern part of Rue du Sentier, near the Bourse, in the second *arrondissement*. He was single and, since he 'would not leave before the end of the month', presumably in employment. No more information is available about him at the age of thirty-four in November 1834. Then, consciously or unconsciously, he took – so far as can be ascertained – the first positive step towards founding his family champagne house. The letter confirming his engagement suggested that, when he was free to travel at the end of the month, he should go to the Hotel d'Espagne in the Rue de Richelieu where he would find 'our assistant director, M. Jacquesson junior' and travel down to Châlons with him. He and Adolphe Jacquesson were almost exactly the same age and a friendship rapidly developed between them; they were to have a considerable effect on one another's lives.

Less than three months after Joseph Krug joined the firm, Maurice Jacquesson died, and Adolphe took control. By the following year the two young men had established a close relationship. Joseph was no longer simply a clerk, but Adolphe Jacquesson's trusted representative, arranging credits, negotiating with clients and merchants as far afield as St Petersburg; and his salary had been increased to 3,000 francs. A few weeks later correspondence shows that he had been admitted to a partnership in the company. Jacquesson wrote, 'The two of us will, I hope, succeed in reaching the objectives we desire. For me, consolidating the firm my father created by so much effort on a more solid base; and for you, dear M. Krug, ensuring for the rest of your days an easy living, associated with the quiet satisfaction of having, through your good advice and efforts, contributed so valuably to the prosperity of the house.' The reply asserts, 'It is too flattering for me, both by virtue of the friendship you are so good as to show me and the evidence of your satisfaction with my poor services. I am overwhelmed and I do not know how to express my gratitude. I shall therefore limit myself, dear M. Jacquesson, to saying – count on me all your life long, and I shall count on you.'

There were problems as the two men strove to extend the scope and size of their business. Their resources could be strained – 'We should not need any credit until October when the *vendange* takes place; but then, the purchase of grapes and, in February and March, buying wine in barrels will demand all our money and all our credit if we are to make a real profit.' In 1839 Jacquesson's agent in the Montagne de Reims wrote – significantly not to Jacquesson but to Joseph Krug – warning him that there were rumours in the vineyards of Verzenay, Verzy and Villers-Marmery that the firm was in financial difficulties and unable to pay for the wines they had ordered. The agent had denied the rumours and wrote 'I have offered to give my signature as guarantee for all you might owe in Verzenay after the vintage.' Though their margins were often finely drawn, the business prospered and grew.

At about this time Adolphe Jacquesson married Louisa Jaunay. She was the younger daughter of François Jaunay – a Frenchman born at Chantilly – and his English wife, née Anne Howell. In 1820 Jaunay was the resident owner of Brunet's Hotel in Leicester Square; he left in 1821, but in 1824 returned to the east side of the Square where he established the double-fronted Jaunay's Hotel at Nos. 25 and 26. He remained there until 1839 when, apparently, the business failed and he emigrated to Australia. The site was then bought, incorporated with No. 27 and opened, in 1854, as The Royal Panopticon of Science and Art – 'to assist by moral and intellectual agencies, the best interests of society'. That worthy project failed. As the Panopticum, it became a waxworks – another failure – before it was converted to the bizarre, Moorish style, Alhambra Palace which for more than seventy years was a popular music hall; though in 1911 the Russian ballet made its highly successful first British appearance there. In 1936 it was demolished to make way for the present Odeon cinema. When François Jaunay left England, his wife went

Joseph Krug I

to live with her daughter, the young Mme Jacquesson, in Châlons-sur-Marne. On 17 February 1841, at the British Embassy in Paris, Joseph Krug married Emma Anne Jaunay – 'spinster of the Parish of St George, Hanover Square, in the county of Middlesex' – the elder sister of Jacquesson's wife. Bishop Luscombe, chaplain to the Ambassador, performed the ceremony and Mme Jacquesson was one of the witnesses. In the marriage settlement agreed at Châlons-sur-Marne on 16 February

Caroline Krug

1841, Mme Krug's *dot* was 25,000 francs; her husband's contribution to the family funds, 85,000 francs – some 25,000 francs inherited from his father, the remainder, his savings. On 3 January of the following year, their only child, Paul Krug, was born.

The situation seemed ideal, especially by nineteenth-century bourgeois standards. Two sisters, both happy mothers, living near their own mother, were married to two men apparently happily associated in a prospering business. Then, in September 1842, to the surprise of everyone else in the two households, Joseph Krug announced his intentions of leaving both the house of Jacquesson and Châlons-sur-Marne. It was the most traumatic act in the history of the family, for close unity and community of interest are strong Krug characteristics.

It was also the crucial event in the creation of the champagne house of Krug. Yet no phase of the family history is less clear nor, for that reason, more compelling of examination and conjecture. On the surface it would need a violent difference to break up such a family group. Here were two friends working together in the same developing firm which one controlled with the other as a welcomed and diligent junior partner. They were married to sisters who, in a foreign country, found comfort in their own company and that of their mother and children. The issue which prompted the separation, whether actual or – possibly – a pretext, is nowhere to be discovered. The evidence provided by correspondence is scanty and one-sided, but not negligible. There was, for instance, a difference of opinion on technical grounds. It seems slight in relation to family unity, but many such splits are caused by emotive reactions to trifling matters.

Although Joseph Krug had been appointed as a clerk in the firm of Jacquesson, he was frequently away from Châlons for weeks at a time, travelling up and down Europe, interviewing agents, dealers and customers. In one letter, despite the Christian name terms and the protestations of affection, he made a firm, positive commercial criticism of Jacquesson – 'This wine is not quite so good as those of Schneider, Heidsieck or Lambry for those three firms have established a vogue here for the $3\frac{1}{2}$ per cent wine which is the strongest. People do not want to pay more than two thalers a bottle. When you prepare new blends you must think of improving the $3\frac{1}{2}$ per cent wines. Competition is frightening and I anticipate we shall achieve nothing except by becoming outstanding for excellent wine and paying particular attention to bottling and an even foam.' Daumer, the experienced German agent, confirmed his judgement in stronger terms – 'Artach of Jagor is not happy with the wines I sent: they are too dull and too sweet – the Hotel de Russie said the same about the last shipment. You have no idea how low this wine is in foam. It is far less than sparkling, which is not liked anywhere, and least of all in Saxony, whose people demand cheerful wines with plenty of foam. I would implore you to support me and to make business a little less difficult for me here by serving well. . . . You gave very good service in the spring . . . If you will do as well with the autumn shipment your reputation will be con-solidated, in spite of all the slander and gossip.'

This should not have proved a fundamental difference between the two men at Châlons: perhaps Krug was simply uttering a self-interested warning. However that may be, it reveals the undoubted fact of his preoccupation with the style and quality of champagne.

The separation, like most within families, was agonized: indeed, the feelings it aroused still lingered in the Krug family more than a century later. Unlike many such differences, however, it was not created in the heat of argument.

There was clearly a disagreement – if not a quarrel –

between the two; and Krug had previously considered leaving. He announced his decision, though, presumably after consideration, in a letter to Jacquesson contained in one to his wife. Adolphe, who had been ill, had gone to Paris for medical treatment and the two sisters and his children went with him. There is no copy of Krug's letter, nor of any response from Adolphe. His wife, Emma's reply, however, still exists; and it is a moving document:

Paris, 29 August 1842

    My dear Krug,

I received your letter just as we were leaving for church and, before reading mine, I handed over the one addressed to Adolphe. If I had imagined what it contained, I assure you I should not have given it to him. I cannot tell you what sorrow your decision has caused him. You had been talking of leaving for a long time, but I confess that I always hoped the matter would resolve itself. Now it has become serious, I assure you I am most sad. When I think of leaving mother, Louisa, and the children to whom, as you know, I am so attached, I cannot believe it possible. Such a separation seems to me like a death: and that it should be deliberate, and on our part, saddens me. Poor Adolphe was even more ill yesterday. He will do anything to make us happy. If office work does not agree with your health, go away more often; he does not ask you to work, take two or three people if necessary to do the work. Only supervise. Be fully the master. Now that M. Schuldheess is leaving, this seems an ideal time to put everything in order and manage the office completely in your own way, with new personnel. You will not be hindered. Do not think that Adolphe has persuaded me to write to you. I can see that the thought of your departure causes him such sorrow, but he does not want to make you stay against your will, despite his wish that we should all stay together. I told him I should write to you, but I have not acquainted him with your letter. Louisa would be so upset to see little Paul leave. Now, Krug, I promise I shall no longer complain about Châlons. We shall make a little journey together. Every year you will go and take the waters; you will consult M. Boniface who will restore your health. We shall all be happy. If you could see Adolphe you would not doubt his attachment to you, and to me also, which must please you, as we are one only. I am very happy that my Paul is well. His rash causes me no anxiety at all; I think it comes from his teething. Were it to continue we could take him with us next month. Do not scold me: I have spent a lot of money on a bed for Paul, but it is very nice and he will be able to use it until he is twelve years old. Now, my dear, decide to remain. Put everything on my back. Say it is for me. Forget what has happened. Adolphe is quite ready to be our friend. Let this business go no further and let no one know of it at Châlons. He has thought things over a lot. Why worry about creating an establishment? You are not ambitious, and, for myself, I have never complained about my position. We shall be able to save to give Paul a good education. He will have more advantages at home than in some God-forsaken place we might go to and, later, we could set him up better than at present. God preserve him for us. Make me happy by changing your resolution which has been for you, I am sure, a painful one. There is still time for me to enjoy a little of my stay in Paris which, until now, has been filled with sadness.

> *Farewell; we shall stay, shall we not?*
> *Your affectionate wife*
> *Emma*

I send all my love to Mother. Tell her that I shall not buy any material for Paul. I shall make dresses for him with my old ones – shall I not? That will do for the time being, as they have still to be made short. When he is clean and we can make them bigger, I will buy new material.

A few phrases afford clues to the situation. 'You had been talking of leaving for a long time': 'I have not acquainted him [Adolphe] with your letter': and – most significantly – 'Why worry about creating an establishment? You are not ambitious' – all suggest that Joseph Krug wanted to leave Jacquesson and set up on his own; and that he had told his wife as much. Such touches as 'we are one only' and repentance for some grumbles in 'I promise I shall no longer complain about Châlons' emphasize the sincerity and humanity of the letter.

Joseph's reply is not available but he clearly acceded to her request, for she wrote to him 'Thank you, my dear, for saying you will stay if I wish it. That is another proof, and a very great one, of your attachment to me.' The same letter may contain the key to the situation in – 'Yield a little and, instead of regretting that you have not the cellars, think that this will make you freer, and we must confess that Clauzet understands that business better than you do.'

Before September was out, though, he wrote again to insist that he must leave. Again no copy of his letter exists, but Emma's reply does:

30 September 1842

My dear Krug,
I am extremely embarrassed by this sorry business for myself and my people. I am anxious that we should all stay together. Apart from the chances of success in establishing yourself, I still fear the worry and the weight of the responsibilities you would have to bear alone might be harmful to your health, while at present we are assured of our possessions which are ample for our needs and our tastes. I repeat, it would grieve me very much to leave Louisa and my mother, and it would not be very pleasant to go either to a foreign country or some back of

beyond place in Champagne. You ask Adolphe for explanations, and that is precisely what he wants to avoid. He is quite
willing to forget all that has taken place and live happily
together, but never speak of this business any more. I think that
he will stay only two or three days here; he would like to shake
hands with you when he comes back, and that the whole thing
should be forgotten. Do think carefully, my dear Krug, before
taking a positive decision. Is it not preferable to overlook an
unpleasantness and live in peace, I being surrounded by all those
I love, rather than look for troubles and sorrows of the heart?
We shall have a talk and see whether, while you are right, you
could not yield a little for the happiness of being together. I am
delighted with the good news about our angel. Do not chide me
for having spent so much money: the bed, candles, tea, all that
mounts up quickly; but you will see that there is nothing useless
in this, nothing we could have dispensed with. I hope you have
said nothing to Clauzet. It is best that our family matters should
remain unknown to strangers, especially those who live in
Châlons. Clauzet would mention it to his wife and the town
and the places around would speak of nothing else. You know
how I despise them all and the little importance I attach to their
opinions. I only ask of them that they should leave me alone,
and that is why I am keen that they should be ignorant of all that
concerns us.

I kiss mother with all my heart, as well as yourself, my good
husband. Adolphe is better. The only skin trouble that he has
left is almost cured. God will that all this should settle down and
that you should be happy. It seems to me that it is a lesson to me,
to show me that I could be sadder than in Châlons. If you stay
we should amuse ourselves with a few little trips. When Paul is
older, he will come with us, and we shall be happy, and
especially together and at peace.

Yours ever,

Your affectionate wife,

Emma

Here the key passages are, first – 'Apart from the chances of success in establishing yourself, I still fear the worry and weight of responsibility you would have to bear alone' which again points to Krug's ambition to set up his own business. 'You are right', however, suggests that Emma, at least, did not think the difference with Jacquesson solely a pretext for leaving.

This time he did not yield. There is no further evidence on the matter from any of the parties concerned.

The temptation to speculate on Joseph's reactions and motives is irresistible. Some other points in the story are not explained, but by comparison with this, they are unimportant. This was the decision which made the house of Krug possible. Until then it was improbable. Indeed, the fact that the three Jaunay women and his and Jacquesson's children were all together in Châlons-sur-Marne made it improbable that Joseph would ever leave the comfortable niche Adolphe Jacquesson had provided. If he stayed, he would never be more than a relatively junior, though comfortable, partner in that firm. If he left, the chances lay between a house of his own and failure. That, according to Emma, Adolphe wanted to avoid explanations and wished never to speak of the matter any more seems to indicate a feeling of guilt on his part. Since she concedes to Joseph 'you are right', it is odd that she did not preserve his letters as she did on other subjects. Hers have survived because he – feeling he was in the right? – kept them. He died first, so Emma was in a position to decide what should be preserved. Family tradition – which is always strong, if not objective – is that Joseph behaved cruelly to his wife in this matter.

Apart from Krug the only people with sufficient knowledge of the original disagreement to pass down an opinion about it were Emma, her sister, her mother and Adolphe Jacquesson – all of whom were, presumably, of a like mind. It is clear that Emma was discontented – possibly homesick for England where she had been brought up – 'It seems to me that it is a lesson to me, to show me that I could be sadder than in Châlons.' In that case, the thought of being far away from her mother and sister, instead of a near neighbour, must have been a dismaying prospect. Was Emma – as two of the letters hint – something of a malcontent? Although the rest of her family were there, she strongly disliked Châlons and – sweepingly – all its people ('You know how I despise them all' is not generous language). Only she can have established the enduring idea in the Krug family that Joseph cruelly caused her unhappiness, and she can only have established it through Paul, who was a year old at the time – not old enough to observe, assess or remember for himself. No word exists of Joseph's side of the affair. Yet she did agree 'you are right' – and he did succeed; established her and Paul in prosperity, and enabled her to see much of her family.

Joseph's second decision to leave may mean that, rethinking, he decided the difference between the two men was too fundamental for them to continue in business together.

The strongest possibility – which would establish a pattern in all that happened – must be that Emma was wrong when she wrote 'You are not ambitious'. It seems that Joseph *was* ambitious; *did* want the cellar – and wanted

Emma Krug

to found a champagne house. If not, the events that followed were indeed an odd series of coincidences.

The possibility that Joseph used some dispute with Adolphe as a justification for setting up on his own is strengthened by the fact that there was no enduring rift between the two families. For many years amiable letters passed between them. A deep affection existed between Paul and his uncle and aunt; while a letter of 1844 – only two years after the separation – indicates a fairly rapid renewal of regard between Joseph Krug and Adolphe Jacquesson. In matters of business, however, the split was complete and final.

The house of Jacquesson went steadily on. It took orders for a million bottles at the Universal Exhibition of 1867 and, in the same year, the Queen of Holland made an official visit to the cellars of Châlons.

In 1871 Adolphe Jacquesson wrote a letter to Paul Krug I – who had then succeeded to the control of the Krug business – which provides a happy postscript to the earlier dispute.

London, 6 April 1871

My dear Paul,
Your mother sent us your good news. We are glad to hear that Caroline and yourself are in good health and that our dear little Joseph is happily growing up.

Our return will be somewhat delayed by a matter proposed to us after your departure. Some reliable businessmen and investors, including M. Bass, the important brewer, are proposing to form a company which would manufacture champagne wines together with beer; the wine business would be carried on and a big brewery would be built. I am roughly in agreement on the price of transfer.

Three of the interested people, together with an engineer and a brewer, are leaving next Monday to visit the establishment.

I shall keep you informed about the whole thing. So far, you are the only one to whom I have spoken about it.

In the hope it will succeed, I kiss the three of you with all my heart.

Adolphe Jacquesson

That development did not take place; although the brewery – la Comète – was built in the next street, Jacquessons had no interest in it. By coincidence, though, in 1972, Edward Young, a subsidiary of the brewing house of Bass Charrington, undertook the British agency for Krug champagne.

With Adolphe's death in 1875, the male line of the Jacquessons ended and the business passed to the de Tassigny family on the female side. In 1925 the firm of Veuve Bur bought its name and transferred it to Reims.

The former considerable area of the establishment in Châlons is occupied by Rue Jacquesson and the crescent called Rue Canal Jacquesson which are now divided between the brewery of la Comète and the houses of railway workers. Parts of the great cellars were taken over by the ordnance section of the French Army and others by the brewery.

Wittingly or not, Joseph Krug made the right decision when he settled in Reims instead of Châlons-sur-Marne. In the 1830s Reims had a population of 35,000, and sustained twenty listed champagne houses; Châlons with 12,000 people had seven, two of them – Perrier et Fils and Jacquesson – of some importance. By 1862 there were thirty-eight houses in Reims – at least a dozen of them large – to thirteen – all the others appreciably less significant than Perrier – in Châlons.

Now Reims is a major champagne town and Châlons, which has prospered in other directions, is not. The explanation is that Châlons originally became a wine town because there were a number of vineyards in the vicinity. They were, though, so near the river and on such unfavourable slopes, as to be more vulnerable to the destructive spring frosts than those in other districts. Gradually, they ceased to be viable and the majority were turned over to other purposes. So, in the nineteenth century, before the introduction of the internal combustion engine, the town was uneconomically farther from the chief vineyards than Reims and Epernay. For the developing trade in sparkling blended champagne, quick transport of the *must* to the makers' cellars was so essential that it was more convenient for newcomers to settle nearer the main vineyards.

Whether Joseph Krug calculated this trend, merely guessed right, or went to Reims by the chance of opportunity, will never be known. Whatever the reason, he did well: though, in 1843, that was only a matter of hope and confidence.

The founding of the House

In October 1842, when he left the employment of Jacquesson et Fils, Joseph Krug was almost forty-two years old. He had some limited capital; nine years' experience of the champagne trade; a wife and a baby son; and the ambition to start a business career in the competitive commerce of a strange city. He knew that, at his age, he had little time to spare if he were to make a fortune. He may have taken some comfort from the number of German names in the champagne trade in Reims – Roederer, Mumm, Walther, Heidsieck, Boden and Ohaus. He cannot have known, though, that he was to prove fortunately to be a child of his age – the first champagne age. The *réduction François* had followed better glass, corks and the *dégorgement* process to make possible the consistent production of clear, sparkling champagne in bottles which, because they rarely burst, reduced wastage and, therefore, the selling price. France's foreign markets, especially Germany, Britain and the United States of America, were industrially flourishing and financially affluent. Britain, too, had repealed the savage tax on French wines and lifted George II's century-old ban on imports of wine in bottle. So the situation was perfect for an immense advance in the production and sale of the wine. Moreover – and conclusively – world fashion confirmed the taste for champagne.

In the twenty-three years between 1843 when Joseph Krug set up in business in Reims, and 1866 when he died, the international market in sparkling champagne rose to an amazing peak.

In that period the output of the Champagne vineyards rose from six million to fifteen million bottles; and export sales trebled from four to twelve million. The entire pattern of champagne production and sales was re-volutionized. First, the balance of the region's output changed so radically that still wine fell from the major to quite a minor proportion of the production. Secondly, fashionable taste dictated a change from a sweet to a substantially dry flavour. This was the rising tide of fortune and Joseph Krug was ready and equipped to be carried along by it.

That must have seemed a distant prospect to him as 1842 passed into 1843. He had not sufficient money, reputation nor influence to command an appreciable position in a business. He had really only himself to sell: and it took him a year to negotiate that to his satisfaction. Hyppolite de Vivès was a wine merchant of some standing in Reims in 1842, when his house was one of only eight in the city that employed more than ten men. About the end of that year he decided to withdraw from any active part in the business while continuing to share its profits as a sleeping partner. He set out to find someone who would be responsible both for day-to-day running and policy decisions.

The eagerness of de Vivès to make him the managing partner in his firm is a considerable compliment to Joseph Krug's ability. The fact is, though, that the two were by no means strangers; de Vivès knew the man he was persuading to join him. 'I hope you will see in my reply a further proof of the great keenness I have always shown to establish relations between us.'

Once the partnership agreement between these two men was signed, the remaining story of the house of Krug is plotted in its ledgers and minutes; motivation is apparent in production, sales figures, purchases and trading decisions. The last doubt, and consequent temptation to speculate, lies in this stage, the final steps to the formation of the company. The surviving correspondence is one-sided – all from de Vivès – but it shows that agreement was not achieved easily. Almost a year after it was reached, however, Joseph Krug wrote de Vivès a letter which explains much.

M. H Vivès
Local   *Reims, 24 August 1844*

Further to our verbal agreement, and in consideration of the difficulties that have arisen regarding the work since 1840, you have kindly agreed to grant a 10 per cent allowance on the amount of these wines, amounting to 140,274.05 francs, ie an allowance of 14,027.40 francs, with which we are debiting your current account with us as on 31 December next. Will you please make the appropriate entry in your books.

On the same day he received the reply:

M. Krug in Reims   *24 August 1844*

I am in agreement with the contents of your letter of today. I have credited your account with the amount of 14,027.40 francs as the allowance agreed between us, on the 1840 wines that I have sold to the Company.

If Joseph had been working for de Vivès since 1840, and now received a 10 per cent allowance on the price of the sleeping partner's 1840 wines, the conclusion must be that he blended for him. 'Work' is a wide term. If it had not been so specifically tied to the value of those wines it might be assumed that he had rendered de Vivès some service – representing or selling for him in the course of his travels. The strict basing of the payment on the value of the 1840 wines sold to the company, however, leaves room for no other conclusion than that Joseph Krug blended those *cuvées* for him. That might explain the rift with Jacquesson, who would hardly have approved of his employee working for a competitor. It would stretch assumption into the realm of guessing to accept that as the cause of their disagreement. It does, though, establish beyond reasonable doubt Joseph's ambition for the cellars, and for a career as a champagne maker in his own right.

It would account, too, for the nature of the negotiations with de Vivès. The discussions were drawn out for almost a year and at times threatened to break down altogether. Joseph drove a stern bargain; often it seems that he 'played hard to get'. The stakes were high, for what he was offered was a business far bigger than his financial resources could command – and complete control of it. He made quite certain of that: in an early letter de Vivès writes 'I have told you that, if I were to keep the entire responsibility of the business it would be impossible for me to give up the high management (as is my wish).'

Although time was not on his side, Joseph was not to be hurried into a decision. At one juncture de Vivès wrote – 'I thank you for the frankness of your reply which shows me you have not entirely given up the idea of our project; though, in view of your uncertainty, you are willing to put me in touch with a reliable person who would meet my needs as you know them.' There were, too, other setbacks. Another letter from de Vivès says 'You were good enough to go into details with regard to the regrettable publicity our projects have had. Do believe that I never supposed you were the source of that publicity. When I was unable to reply that these rumours were unjustified, I was no longer worried about them on your account or mine. I accept very willingly, especially in view of the difficulties you envisage, that you will probably have taken a decision before you meet the other person.'

Towards the end of the exchanges he takes a firm line – 'Your reply to my proposals surprises me, especially since it departs entirely from our early talks and your last proposals. I sincerely wonder whether we could agree for, while you have always found me ready to act generously for mutual understanding, it is impossible for me to assume commitments too expensive for me. However, since I have always hoped not to be the one to close the matter, I will give you an example of the kind of concession which ought to decide you if you will want to conclude this business. . . . I agree to raise my investment to 260,000 francs in the light of your third of 130,000 francs, although this departs so far from my original intentions that my commitment is more or less doubled. Concerning the wines, there is an enormous difference between my calculations and my estimate and yours; but to remove that difficulty I will accept the price you name but set the due date at June 1844 instead of December 1844 as you propose. This is the item to which I am most opposed – why do you ask me for 6,000 francs when you have a 33 per cent interest and when you ask only 4,000 francs with a 10 per cent interest?' Even that did not conclude the issue. When, eventually, the company was formed, in November 1843, Joseph had won himself a 50 per cent interest (from 10 per cent) and an annual salary of 3,000 francs, plus expenses of 1,000 francs. He could hardly have hoped to do better – few realists would have expected quite so much.

Because French law did not allow a firm to carry the name of a sleeping partner, de Vivès left it to the active member to give it 'a name you regard as suitable in the interest of the business'. Joseph Krug called it Krug et Cie. The firm took over de Vivès' entire trading stock of wines, spirits, cellar equipment, bottles, labels, wine-making equipment and materials – at Joseph's valuation of 324,972 francs.

The inventory of de Vivès' stock shows him to have been far more of a general wine merchant than a modern champagne house. He had, of course, the usual still wines of Champagne. The name of Sillery occurs in all the wine

histories and the sales lists of the first three-quarters of the nineteenth century. Its high reputation in other countries was based on at least two different wines. First there was the output of the village of Sillery which was, and still is, of high quality. Then, even more esteemed in the region, were the wines of the Brulart family who became the Marquesses of Sillery. They had extensive vineyards both there and in Verzenay but all their wine, from either village, was called Sillery. A long line of members of the family held high office under the French crown, they were wealthy and they spent without stint on the vineyards that

were their pride (their crest was wine casks entwined with vines). Their still wine was recognized for years as outstanding; it was popular at the French court, and certainly in England. The last Marquis went to the guillotine during the Revolution, and the vineyards were subsequently divided among many owners. By the end of the nineteenth century, the Brulart Sillery was a rarity.

The de Vivès stocks included wines of Ay and Verzenay; single and blended wines of the area of 'Clairette'; 'Xeres de Rivart'; the suspicious-sounding 'Porto de Cette' and 'Porto de Rouen'; old Frontignac

wine; Malvoisie; Madeira; and a *teinte* – a wine used to colour others – from Fismes, about twenty kilometres west of Reims, not now a wine-growing area. There were 550 kilogrammes of candles – to light the cellars – and 115 kilogrammes of string, some 70,000 corks, 800 bottles and 920 empty casks.

The cellar and offices of Krug et Cie, rented from de Vivès, were at No 8 Rue St Hilaire, where that quiet street gives on to the Place Leon Bourgeois, no more than two or three minutes' walk from the present Krug establishment. Their neighbours were Roederer and Werlé-Clicquot. In 1843 the premises consisted of three tiers of cellars under the offices. Joseph I lived a few metres away in Place de l'Hôtel de Ville, on a site now overlaid in a changed street-plan. In 1930, nearly sixty years after the firm had moved to its present premises, Joseph Krug II bought back the cellars at 8 Rue St Hilaire from their then owner, Frederic Bouchard, to store his stocks of the 1928 and 1929 vintages; and Paul II only sold them again – to building developers – in the 1950s. In 1971 a block of tidily anonymous white flats was built on the site with underground garages for the tenants in the former cellars.

The firm's files show a wide variety of labels in those early days, many, no doubt, carried over from de Vivès. By coincidence, some, including a 'Champagne Mousseux; Grand Vin de Bouzy' and an 'Ay Mousseux, Premier Quality', bear the name of Emma's brother; 'Louis Jaunay, Reims'. Jaunay was later to become a neighbour as *'Association Vinicole de Champagne'*. There was Sillery Mousseux, Bouzy, and Ay Mousseux – unblended wines – and 'Oeil de Perdrix' – 'partridge eye' – the pinkish wine which, at that time, was often produced from the black grapes of the region. Two *crémant* or 'creaming' wines – not to be confused with the Champagne vineyard village of Cramant – less sparkling than a *mousseux,* came from Ay and Sillery.

Now Joseph Krug had control of a champagne house with stock and capital. Again there is evidence that he did want a cellar; did want to blend. At the outset of their negotiations, eight months before the partnership was agreed, a letter from de Vivès told him 'Today I sent to the address you gave me in Mainz the twelve bottles of 1840 wine blended as agreed; I enclose a note of the numbers of the bottles used so that you can see how they were composed.'

Immediately, though, he threw himself into the matter of selling wine. The firm's great folio ledgers – all uniformly bound in green goat-skin and brass by Gaymond et Gerault, and kept in exactly the same way for over a century – show the extent of his trading. Joseph Krug I could certainly speak, read and write German, French and English; and he could make himself understood – and sell wine – in Russia. In 1844 the firm sold 25,000 bottles through Chapman and Warren in Rio de Janeiro; nearly 2,000 to Holler in Mainz; 14,000 to Hedadt in New York; 12,000 to Ashby and Charles Cock in London; 2,000 to Witt in St Petersburg. In the following year new accounts were opened with Bicker and Moddemann of Amsterdam; Voelker in Valparaiso; Brandt of Arkansaw; agencies were established in New Orleans, Martinique, Bahia, Madras, Calcutta, Malta.

Joseph Krug supervised the administration, but in 1844 Henri Soullié joined the firm as chief clerk with responsibility for French correspondence and book-keeping. His starting salary of 1,200 francs a year, rising by annual increments of 100 francs, contrasts sharply with Joseph Krug's 2,000 francs, increased in a year to 3,000 francs, of a decade earlier. Soullié was to become one of the characters and traditionalists of the house of Krug.

In the spring of 1845 Joseph made his first blend for Krug et Cie: four *cuvées* – called prosaically enough, A, B, C and D – in 40,842 bottles which sold at 1.45 francs each. In the following year Krug et Cie bought their own grapes for the first time, a substantial amount of them from Bouzy, and Joseph Krug – unknowingly but, surely, in heart and ambition – founded the family tradition of champagne blending.

Soon, though, less pleasing matters weighed on him. Some years later, Paul I, an accomplished penman, compiled a chart of *The Results of the Operations of Maison Krug* which lays out the relevant figures in immaculate script and with admirable clarity. It is a record of effort and enterprise but certainly not of unbroken success. The statistics emphasize the vulnerability of the company on several grounds. In the first place it has never been large, in strict size, or wealth – by comparison with the combine-owned houses – or in width of operation. It has not in modern times produced more than half a million bottles in a year (481,926 bottles in 1973 is the most in the post-war period). Sometimes in the last century wine blended for other houses took the total higher: but the 618,260 bottles of 1909 is the highest annual figure for Krug champagne. It has, too, always aimed at a high quality product, ideally, a single wine in any year.

Finally it has always relied largely on exports for its business. Up to 1920 nearly 99 per cent of the firm's champagne was exported. In France it was sold only to a few major hotels and restaurants – for travellers who drank it habitually in their own countries – but the only private customers were members of the family and a few friends. Despite the post-war increase in French champagne consumption and purchasing power, which has resulted in half all the champagne sold being drunk in France, the Krug export figure has only twice fallen below 70 per cent of their total sales (68.56 per cent in 1971 and 68.01 per cent in 1974).

While this has made for prestigious and often highly-priced sales, it has left the firm at the mercy of many outside influences.

Paul's survey shows some harsh setbacks. Sales increased rapidly at first; the 90,382 bottles of 1844 rose in the three succeeding years to 109,088, 124,924, and then 151,245. Profits went up in those first three years, from 4,078 francs to 20,000 francs to 24,454 francs. In 1847, however, despite the highest sales figure, they fell to 8,097 francs and, in 1848, although production was as high as 117,851 bottles, the house of Krug made a shattering loss of 52,916 francs – almost equivalent to their entire profits of the four preceding years. In the 'observations' column Paul I wrote simply 'Revolution'. The firm could absorb the blow, but not a repetition of it. On 6 December 1846 the *Préfect* of the Marne dispatched to 'Citizen Krug, Wine Merchant of Reims' (now Jean-Joseph Krug) a naturalization certificate granting him the privileges of a French citizen. The covering letter hoped it would reach him in time for him to vote in the forthcoming elections. The elections were held on 10 December 1846. Was he one of the electors who gave Louis Napoleon his overwhelming majority?

The loss of 1848 was almost exactly balanced by a profit of 51,925 francs in the following year; and, although sales fell to 98,519 bottles in 1850, the profit rose to 55,671 francs.

A revealing and probably formative phase in the history of the house of Krug occurred in 1851. The agreement between the partners specifically forbade Joseph to undertake work for any other wine house. A letter from de Vivès gave him permission to make a *tirage* outside the confines of the company in 1851, adding – 'In this circumstance as always, I rely upon your usual caution and *savoir faire*.' For the first time, Paul's table records wines '*Ventes sur place*' – simply enough, wine made for, or sold to, other shippers. The highest compliment a blender can be offered is to be paid to blend champagne for a competitor. The *tirage* amounted to 172,000 bottles and pushed the firm's profits up to 86,574 francs for the year. That was a poor (1850) vintage. So were the next four, '51, '52, '53, and '54. In a poor year only an outstanding maker can produce even a passable champagne. In those four years Joseph Krug directed the blending of almost a million bottles of champagne – two-thirds of them went to other shippers – and the firm's annual profits averaged 135,000 francs. In 1855 the value of the wine in the cellars of Krug et Cie was 837,661.58 francs: de Vivès' holding in the company was 536,826 francs, Joseph Krug's 422,199 francs.

The 1855 vintage was only middling: in 1856 Joseph made 500,915 bottles from it, 422,465 bottles for other houses; and opened an account with the Bank of France. The 1856 vintage was good; the 1857 Krug sales, at 66,082 bottles, were the lowest in the firm's history. Paul's review notes, laconically, 'commercial crisis in Europe and America'. Since these were the firm's main markets, the figure might have been even lower: but profits were down to 1,055 francs. Nevertheless, in those two years Joseph blended the splendid 1856 vintage and the superlative 1857 which were later to do the firm immense credit. So at the end of 1857 he could write 'the tide has turned'. Surely enough, although the crisis continued, there was a slight upturn to 129,930 bottles by the following December.

It must be remembered that the Krug champagnes were being sold from three to six years after the vintage. The economy of wine-production is precarious and often fierce. The best of *vignerons* can have a fortune's worth of fine, well-made wine in his cellars yet face the alternatives of a crippling lack of working capital, or having to borrow at savage interest rates. In 1860 – with the indifferent 1859s – Joseph made 114,000 bottles for his competitors, and the firm showed a profit of 164,402 francs.

No sooner was the House apparently re-established on that high level of prosperity than, in 1861 and 1862, it fell into two years of losses – 59,009 francs and 23,211 francs – explained by the American Civil War. Everyone re-trenched: over the two years the firm's blending revenue dropped by 60 per cent.

Krug have often exaggeratedly reflected the state of the champagne industry: and certainly they seem to have done so here. According to Vizetelly, quoting official returns of the Chamber of Commerce of Reims, in his *Facts About Champagne* (1879) total champagne sales showed a small fall in 1848; an increase in 1857; a 12 per cent drop in 1858 and a small one in 1861, one of 16 per cent in 1862.

For more than a century from 1843 when Joseph Krug opened his business in Reims, the major proportion of the steadily increasing production of champagne was sold to other countries – especially Britain, the United States of America and Russia. In the nineteenth century all the champagne shippers – Krug particularly – wooed the British and American markets assiduously. The creation of popular markets there accounts for the fact that, in the middle of the nineteenth century, Krug appeared under some labels unthinkable to its present-day purism.

For the home trade the titles were orthodox. The 1857 vintage Sillery label was not unlike the standard present day design; while in 1861 there was for the first time a *Private Cuvée*. Verzenay Mousseux, Verzenay Grand Mousseux, Sillery Grand Mousseux, Crême de Bouzy;

EXTRA DRY FOR INVALIDS

K & C°

Rheims.

Joseph Paul et Cie; Carte Blanche (1865); Fleur de Sillery, Gout Français (with a French tricoleur) and Oeil de Perdrix – and the Tisane de Champagne made for Louis Jaunay – were all of a kind the French buyer knew.

So, for the overseas market were Private Quality, First Quality, Second Quality, 'Extra'. There was mild concession in 'English Taste' (decorated with a Red Ensign), 'Extra Dry for Invalids (joyous thought – for invalids).

Early versions of the 'BOB' – buyer's own brand – bore the names of many English merchants such as Frederick Sawyer 'Crystal Palace'; Dry Champagne for Page and Sandeman, London; David Sandeman and Co, Preston; International Exhibition, 1862; and Imperial Rosé.

For the United States of America there was one label decorated with the head of George Washington and the American eagle; Missouri Brand; Bonanza; *Gout Americain*. There was, too, for the pleasure of those building or

sustaining the British Empire overseas, 'Sparkling Dry
Sillery, Extra Quality', specially labelled for Murray and
Company, Reserved for India, Lucknow; A Scott and Co,

SPARKLING DRY SILLERY.
EXTRA QUALITY.

Specially selected for
MURRAY & C⁰.,
LUCKNOW.

Reserve for India.

Rangoon; Joseph Travers and Co, Singapore and Penang; or for the French, *Compagnie de Commerce et de Navigation,* Saigon and Haiphon.

The problem of meeting the export market was not merely one of label but of taste, price and tariff. We have seen that, as early as 1841, Joseph Krug was pressing Adolphe Jacquesson for a better $3\frac{1}{2}$ per cent wine for Germany. Yet at the same time the Russian trade, which he had also to meet, demanded an almost impossibly sweet blend with a dosage of as much as 16 per cent. That market was created during the Russian military occupation of the Reims area by the Russian forces under Wolkonski after Waterloo. The officers of that army took back champagne to their own country which, until the Revolution of 1917, was second only to Britain as an importer of champagne. Roederer and Clicquot were the major exporters to Russia which may explain the fact that they were the last two houses to ship sweet champagne to England.

The British palate, too, until the 1850s was extremely sweet. In Joseph Krug's career at Reims, the proportion of champagne exported rose from 50 per cent to 75 per cent of a production more than doubled. In England by the 1850s the still wines of Champagne were passing out of favour and the most popular taste was for the sparkling as sweet as a 15 per cent dosage could make it. The wine was generally at least yellow in colour, often amber brown or 'partridge eye', conveying an impression of richness and power. Often, to the horror of the French, British drinkers added brandy to their champagne. The change in fashion was rapid, but also erratic. As early as 1846 the London firm of Burne, Turner shipped a pure *brut* champagne; but

their customers – members of a services club – rejected it. In 1850 an eminent Reims shipper refused to supply a *brut*.

After 1865 wines of the leading shippers were generally 5 per cent with virtually only the Russian market above 10 per cent. By then most of the Reims, Epernay and Ay shippers made specific 'English *cuvées*' substantially drier than their blends for France or for other export markets. This may have been largely a London demand: since Barwells, with shops in Norwich and London, sold sweet champagne in their Norwich establishment until far into the twentieth century; while even in 1868, Chavasse imported a wine of 16 per cent dosage from George Goulet of Reims.

Krug inclined towards the dry taste in their plan for the British market, which included, of course, the British overseas, in India, south-east Asia, China, Australia and military and naval establishments round the world.

The partners constantly revised their agreement; Joseph Krug's share of the profits – or losses – rose from 50 per cent to 72 per cent and on to 75 per cent. Meanwhile de Vivès could be content that, while his percentage decreased, the growth in the firm's profits generally ensured that the amount he received also grew.

One significant amendment to the deed of the company was made in 1863:

1   Notwithstanding the disposition of that article No. 18 providing that during the three years which precede the expiry of the company, he will not be allowed to make purchases other than for his necessities and need: It is agreed that Monsieur Krug can continue his specialist operations on account of the business as in the past, until the end of the said company.

2   As it is further stipulated in article No. 18 from the beginning of that same period, M. Krug can make purchases of his own account if they are not set to the account of the said company.

It is also agreed that on each operation on account of the company, Monsieur Krug will be able to reserve one part for his own account at the current price, fixing the quantity before the *tirage* if the wines are in cask, and before the purchase if they are in bottles.

Thus Joseph I was enabled to work on his own account, outside the company – in which, of course, he had to share his profits – solely in his personal interest. Accordingly, in the following spring, de Vivès wrote to him:

Messrs Joseph Krug et Cie
Reims   *Reims, 3 April 1864*

   Dear M. Krug
In your letter you inform me that in accordance with the terms agreed between us on 2 June 1863, you intend to keep on your own account half – both in bottles and half-bottles – each of the growths the House intends to take in this year, as well as of the

wines bought *'en cercles'*, intended for reserve, or increase of *tirage*. You will give me the name of them when the growths are definitely formed.

I have taken good note of these arrangements and I hasten to acknowledge receipt of them.

I am as always,
Yours very sincerely
H Vivès

The export troubles of the champagne houses might have been even more acute during the period of the American Civil War but for the fact that Britain reduced the amount of duty payable. William Ewart Gladstone, the Chancellor of the Exchequer responsible for the Cobden-Gladstone Treaty of 1860, reduced the duty on French wine from 5s 9d to between 1s 0d and 2s 6d a gallon, which meant 5s 0d a dozen for champagne. It was his idea – or ideal – that the working man should be weaned away from the evil of gin, and from the public house, to a domestic supper with a bottle of wine. He failed. The working man continued to drink beer in the pub, while the wealthy stocked their cellars with fine table wines and port – as a recent auction of the nineteenth-century cellar of Gladstone's brother revealed. Gladstone had a reputation as a connoisseur of claret and his tax change created the term 'Gladstone's claret', but he was by no means solely a claret drinker and he is said habitually to have drunk a quart of champagne with his supper. Lord Houghton (Richard Monckton Milnes) official laureate of Grillion's Club, to which W E G belonged, began some verses to him with:

Trace we the workings of that wondrous brain
Warmed by one bottle of our dry champagne.

So long as England remained prosperous, champagne in general, and the house of Krug in particular, also prospered. Prices were competitive. English wine merchants – a type virtually unknown in wine-producing countries – scoured the markets of the world, but especially of France, Portugal, Germany and Spain, for their wares. Their prices were compared: none could afford to be dearer than his neighbour. Krug was never the cheapest champagne, but Joseph kept his prices closely trimmed. In 1843 he charged 2.14 francs a bottle; in 1868, two years after his death, his son's price was 2.27 francs: in the interim it had risen to 2.76 francs (1861) but had been as low as 2.08 francs in 1863.

The last *cuvée* Joseph Krug made was the 1865, blended in the spring of 1866; it was one of the great champagnes of the mid-century.

6

Joseph Krug I

The first Joseph Krug must be remembered primarily as a successful business man. He founded a *grande marque* champagne and made a personal fortune. He was fortunate in his sleeping partner. Hyppolyte de Vivès put up the major proportion of the original capital without which the firm's operations would have been severely handicapped in a period of rapid expansion, but keen competition, in the champagne trade. It seems that de Vivès might almost have been cast, by nature, as a sleeping partner. Through the early history of the firm he is a shadowy figure, making little positive impact. He had made the capture he wanted – of Joseph Krug – and he was content to lapse into the background. He cheerfully acquiesced in his more active partner's ambitious excursions and, on the whole, he profited from them. In the course of the firm's development, his share of the profits – in terms of percentage – decreased: but on the whole it saw a fairly steady increase in actual cash terms. Always courteous and amiable, he remained a friend of the family to his death.

For all Joseph Krug's commercial success and the harsh fashion of his original – and highly effective – bargaining with de Vivès, he seems not to have been a hard man. A photograph confirms the accuracy of the portrait painter in giving him a wide, generous mouth, steady eyes and a generally sensitive and thoughtful expression.

In addition to his business acumen, knowledge of at least three languages and a quality of purpose, he had the even rarer flair for the blending of champagne. Decisively he had the knack of success. It cannot be other than significant that a book about the Reims area published in 1846 – only three years after Krug et Cie was founded – listed a few of the senior champagne houses and then went on 'other well known names are Krug, Delbeck, Lanson et Greno.' So a professional visitor to Reims encountered the name – with a good reputation – of the then youngest house in the city before many of its seniors.

A German married to an Englishwoman, Joseph Krug was building a business in a city he did not know – and where he was not known nor, as yet, accepted: and, at the same time, establishing roots for a family which had none there. He contrived to carry through those operations, so far as can be ascertained, equably.

Joseph was born into a Roman Catholic family in Mainz. His wife, though, was a strict Protestant; Paul was brought up in that faith and he, too, married a convinced Protestant. The rest of the family, down to the present, has been devoutly and devotedly part of the Calvinist community of Reims, several of them members of the church council.

Joseph kept a notebook: it was found after his death by

his son, Paul, who packed it up neatly and put it away among a stack of family documents. It remained there, unknown and unread, until the present incumbent of the house – Paul II – who has a strong bent for history, and especially family history, discovered it and perceived its relevance. He came upon it in the course of patient sifting through an extremely weighty family documentation – which would be even more extensive but for damage and destruction inflicted by the German bombardment of the First World War. Only that delving made the near-continuity of this history possible. Joseph's notebook was essentially personal. Kept in the neatly uniform script of the trained clerk, it begins by setting out the details of his marriage settlement with additions to include his wife's subsequent legacies. It is largely concerned with Joseph I's finances – as distinct from the firm's – and his dealings in land and property. At one point, in 1856, he notes: 'I am not making an entry for my personal possessions since at the moment they are of no appreciable value.' That situation did not last long. It is of some vinous, family, traditional – and even historic – importance, however, that he set down some notes on blending which incorporate the basic theory of the wines his descendants make today.

My opinions on blends (before bottling): and how they should be composed:

1   It is not possible to make a good wine except from good elements – wines from good growths.

    One may obtain a blend of good appearance with mean or mediocre elements and growths but these are

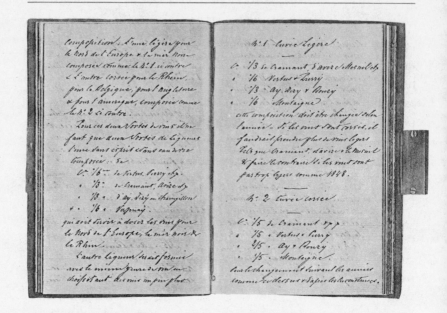

exceptions: one can never rely on them and they put one's whole method and reputation at risk.

2   The greatest care must be taken
    – in making the blend completely homogeneous.
    – in fining, racking and bottling.

In principle, a good house ought to make two similarly composed blends: one light for the north of Europe and the Black Sea countries, the other for the Rhine country, Belgium, England and America.

No 1: light blend
    – $\frac{1}{3}$ Cramant, Avize, Le Mesnil, etc . . .
    – $\frac{1}{6}$ Vertus, Pierry
    – $\frac{1}{3}$ Ay, Dizy, Bouzy
    – $\frac{1}{6}$ Montagne de Reims

This composition can be altered according to the year.

If the wines are full-bodied, one must use more light wines such as Cramant, Avize and Le Mesnil; and the opposite if they are too light like, for instance, those of 1848.

No 2: bodied blend
- $\frac{1}{5}$ Cramant, etc . . .
- $\frac{1}{5}$ Vertus, Pierry
- $\frac{2}{5}$ Ay, Bouzy
- $\frac{1}{5}$ Montagne de Reims

Alterations can be made according to the year as for No 1 and according to circumstances.

The two kinds of wines require two different kinds of liquor; one without any addition of alcohol or spirit composed of:
- $\frac{1}{6}$ Vertus, Pierry, etc . . .
- $\frac{1}{3}$ Cramant, Avize, etc . . .
- $\frac{1}{3}$ Ay, Dizy or Champillon
- $\frac{1}{6}$ Verzenay

This will be used to liquor the wines prepared for the north of Europe, the Black Sea and the Rhône countries. The other liquor should be made with the same kinds of wine but select more full-bodied *cépages*, and add a small dose of fine spirit of cognac at least two years old but not too old.

The second liquor would be composed roughly as follows:
- $\frac{1}{6}$ Vertus, Pierry, etc . . .
- $\frac{1}{6}$ Cramant, Avize
- $\frac{1}{3}$ Ay, Dizy
- $\frac{1}{3}$ Montagne de Reims with the above quantity of spirit

The dose should be 18 litres or 18 bottles per cask of liquor, to sweeten the wine for England and Belgium.

So far as wine exported to America is concerned one could blend the two liquors together using $\frac{1}{3}$ of one and $\frac{2}{3}$ of the other, depending on circumstances.

For the Rhine countries one would take some of the full-bodied blend with the light liquor or the light blend with the full-bodied liquor. This would meet the demand, there, for slightly more full-bodied wine than in Saxe, in the north of Germany, Poland, Russia and Sweden.

In Hamburg the taste is for wines more full-bodied again: eg a light blend with a full-bodied liquor.

It is always a wise precaution to send samples in advance with various doses to ascertain the taste of customers in each country.

The notebook records his purchase of 'the Premises' – presumably No 8 Rue St Hilaire – in 1856; some 16,000 francs spent on 'personal possessions' in the following three years. In 1861 he enters without comment his 72 per cent share of the firm's loss on the year at 42,488 francs; and, in 1862, some 17,400 francs, followed by an increase of capital to 450,000 francs. He buys part of the *Jardin Lelarge* with Louis Jaunay; '*le terrain Bout du Temple*'; 2,321 francs worth of silver plate. He had come a long way in thirty years from Jacquesson's 2,000-francs-a-year clerk at Châlons-sur-Marne.

His feelings towards his son were healthily and affectionately normal with a strong suggestion of the added indulgence generally shown to an only child.

Clearly, he hoped that the boy would follow him into the business of wine which had begun as his ambition and become his achievement. Fortunately for the contentment of both of them – and the future of the House – there was never any real doubt about that. The influence not only of his parents but also of his Jacquesson-Jaunay uncle, aunt and cousins and the de Vivès family ensured that Paul was absorbed into that world of wine. If he ever hesitated he must have been persuaded by observing, closely at hand, the immense and still growing prosperity of those who accepted the kind of position which was his birthright in the hierarchy of champagne.

The family exchanged letters when any of them were away from home which was quite often the case when Paul, as a child, was taken to England and Germany by his mother, or, later, away gaining experience or on the firm's business. Joseph, too, travelled quite extensively. Apart from taking the waters at Carlsbad and conducting Emma to Paris to shop or to visit her dentist, he still maintained contact with the firm's customers in other countries and often took his wife with him. Only two years before his death he wrote from Vienna to M. Soullié in the office – 'Since, from tomorrow, we shall stay nowhere for more than one day, I cannot give you an address; but I shall write to you and give signs of life every two or three days.'

Two fatherly letters written to the fourteen-year-old Paul who was away in England, show something of the character of the most distant member of the House and the one about whom – understandably since he had only one child – few personal or character memories have survived in the family.

Reims, 29 July 1856

My dear Paul,

Your letter of yesterday gave me pleasure; but it would have pleased me more if you had not made so many mistakes, especially errors of negligence, for I am convinced that you know very well that one does not write *shouite* for *souhaite* in '*Je lui souhaite un bonne santé*'; and that one does not say '*nous avons arrivé à Paris*' but '*nous sommes arrivés à Paris*'.

Perhaps you wanted to get it over too quickly. It is better, my boy, to write only one letter carefully than to write two carelessly.

You believe, my dear Paul, that I think you lazy; no, my child, for the moment I look upon you as being on holiday and I hope above all else that you will enjoy your trip. Travel is instructive and this is partly the reason which decided your mother to show you England, the Exhibition and the thousand other interesting things.

If you do not have the time to write to me in Paris, write to me from London, but without rushing, with reflection, so that I can be pleased.

Toni has written a charming letter to Grandmother to give her news of your stay in Châlons. How lucky you were with your fishing: fourteen fish. It is a pity they were not so big as the sole your mother sent us, or they would have provided us with quite a number of dinners.

I hope that you will have seen the eclipse of the sun. The whole of Reims was in the streets, or on the battlements to see this phenomenon. What struck me most was that science was able to calculate within one minute the time it would take place. You can thus see that study is useful. I am happy to learn that you saw two balloons, this is also very interesting.

Pauline is well and her little brother, too. Keep in good health and do not tire yourself too much. Do not be afraid when you cross the Channel to go to Britain. There is not the slightest danger, except that the movement of the ship is unpleasant, and makes quite a number of people ill, but that is over immediately on landing.

Farewell my dear Paul, be kind to your mother and try to please her.

Your affectionate father,
Jos. Krug

Another letter written during the same trip has one passage which the British reader of today must find somewhat naïve – 'You do not tell us anything of Birmingham, yet it is a large industrial town where there must be many things to see. As you do not speak of them in your letters, I hope you will make up for that by long accounts on your return, so be careful, take care to notice everything and forget nothing.' There is an eternally accurate snapshot of the expatriate Englishwoman in – 'Your grandmother asks you to enter sewing cotton in your notebook and remind your mother about it. Grandmother wants mother to bring back as much as possible.' Again, indicative of Paul's later interests and, again, of the close contact the family maintained with the Jaunays – 'The first day of the hunting season is on 7 September and I expect your cousins will be back in Châlons for that day.' Finally, the wine man comes through – 'For several days now we have had fine hot weather. If it continues to the *vendange* we shall have fine grapes and, consequently, good wine.' The weather did hold and this judgement was accurate, the 1856 champagne was a good – but not quite a great – vintage.

Another letter was sent at the end of Paul's visit to England:

Reims, Saturday 13 September 1856

My dear Paul,
Thank you for your good letter of the 11th written after your return from Gravesend. It gives me all the more pleasure for

being well written and because it contains the news that you had a good time on the banks of the Lower Thames; and especially that Mother is happy with you. You cannot know how much pleasure this gives me; so continue to be obedient and behave like a good boy. Take advantage of your last moments in London to have a good look at that great commercial city, so that the impression remains and you can remember later all that you have seen. Your grandmother and I will be delighted to hear your traveller's impressions. Grandmother has not yet written to give you her news, but I shall write to her today to give her yours. Tell your mother that I am very pleased that she used the money for a dress, and that I learn with pleasure she likes the Scottish shawl.

So you are about to leave for home: I am not sorry, for I am beginning to be tired of being alone. I wish you a pleasant crossing, be brave and look after your mother.

If you can arrange to sail so that you do not spend the night at sea I advise you to do so. You will enjoy the country more and also the crossing. . . .

The father-son relationship was soon reinforced by their business life together. In 1863 Joseph, in accordance with a practice quite general in France at the time, paid 2,300 francs to secure Paul's exemption from military service so that he might continue to work in the firm. In the same year he wrote to him from Carlsbad:

Carlsbad, 16 July 1863

My dear Paul,
I have just received your dear letter of 13th instant and thank you for the details you give me about the business, which I see is going well.

I am more or less certain that vintage No 120 will be good – even very good. I learn with pleasure that it is lively and I also hope that it will not be too heavily charged with sediment.

I see that orders are continuing to come in and that the month of August will still not be too bad as regards shipments. I am also pleased to see that Mr Gibbs is taking some 2304 at 34/-. I am sure that he will be happy with it; but regarding the half-bottles for Elliston, it seems to me that the A/58 at $6\frac{1}{2}\%$ is rather heavily blended. However, as there is no red in the liquor, perhaps the blend is exactly as you have indicated. I share your opinion that a shipment of 25 to 30 crates must be put on the road for Vera Cruz. The taking of Mexico will probably revive demand for our article and it is a good thing to have a little of it on the way.

As to the news from New Orleans, it is indeed satisfactory. I think it would be well to have 200 crates for the first opportunity that arises, by a French vessel preferably, but if necessary a neutral ship. If there is no 2304 ready, it may be advisable to take some 455, but only in case of need.

We must accept the pipe of spirit from the firm in Jarnac. The person who came from that firm called with a letter of recommendation from Fould et Cie, and I could not help but give him a little order. It is new spirit which can be compared with a sample from M. de Moers, with his price for comparison; but if there is only a slight difference we shall say nothing.

We must not be surprised that M. Soyez-Moreau does not settle his accounts as quickly as he should: he is not rich and is probably travelling. However, we must write to him again or go to him, and press a little for our money for which we have a use at this time.

I think you did well to write about Paul Dehaitre to M. de Vivès. I hope you gave him our news at the same time.

We are well and greet you as well as M. Soullié very heartily.

J J Krug

The most revealing passages are those least characteristic of a man who put the material side of business first. One is 'I could not help but give him a little order': the other, 'We must not be surprised that M. Soyez-Moreau does not settle his accounts as quickly as he should: he is not rich and is probably travelling.' Those are the reactions of a generous man.

The 'taking of Mexico' he refers to was the appalling error of the French invasion ordered by Napoleon III, who installed the Austrian Archduke Maximilian as Emperor of Mexico. The undertaking failed; Maximilian misjudged the situation and, opposed by the United States of America and renounced by France, he was overthrown and executed. It was a tragic phase, too brief – only three years – to make any lasting impact on history.

Another letter of the same year, written when Joseph had taken Emma to Paris where 'she is happy with her dentist who does not keep her too long' – is all the shrewd *négociant* to his junior partner. 'You mention a firm of S . . . et J . . ., enquiring about wine export prices. Let us hope this is not a trap set for us. Possibly you will have written to London for information about them and the lines in which they operate. . . .' 'The weather becoming cold again gives me every reason to believe that the wines in the cellars will not go forward very fast and that we shall, therefore, be in control of the situation.' 'Yesterday I had a long talk with M. Meletta. He and M. Lafitte are anxious that their successor should keep up the sale of our wines in New York. M. Meletta said "I am convinced that if Messrs I. I. impose higher prices they will gain little and consequently competition between New York and New Orleans will die out." I replied to him "My dear M. M, that would be the safest and most reliable way of achieving so desirable an end." '

The last entry Joseph Krug I ever made in his notebook set out his financial position at the end of December 1865 when he calculated his personal fortune at 1,407,921 francs.

Beneath that his son wrote 'My poor father died this year on 5 August at Allevard. The division of his fortune between my mother and myself took place on 16 August and the new commercial company was formed on 1 September 1866.' Then he wrapped up the notebook and put it away in the family files where it remained unopened for a hundred years.

7

The making of a marque

With the second phase of the family it is possible to walk on firm ground. There was too much uncertainty in the career of the first Joseph for the firm's course to be plotted with real certainty. He provided the House with a foundation so well planned and soundly established that it required only reasonable management for a prosperous future. The Krug family legend tends to give the major credit for success to Paul I; that is not unreasonable. The fairer judgement is that Joseph I provided a basis from which success was probable and that Paul I established that probability, and did so in the most handsome fashion. His image within the family is one of splendour. He is entitled to it; but he himself would no doubt give considerable credit to his father. The temptation to be resisted is to allocate degrees of merit in what has been so unfalteringly a family operation. In truth it has been a progression shaped by the coincidence of historic opportunity with the presence, in the right place, of people capable of taking it. In short, there was a world demand for champagne and, even before it was fully voiced, Joseph Krug had aspired to meet it and equipped himself to do so. Although he died before it reached its peak, he had trained and established his son to exploit it fully.

If we are to make a distinction – as opposed to comparison – between their contributions it must be that, apart from creating the firm, Joseph I made and sold good champagne; Paul I made and sold Krug champagne. It was he who effectively created the *marque*, made Krug champagne not simply a good, but a prestigious – élite – champagne; or, both literally and figuratively, he translated it from a *marque* to a *grande marque*.

The first Paul Krug was even more fortunate than his father in the circumstances and time of his birth. He was twenty-four years old when, in 1866, he took over a firmly established champagne house. He had, too, the happy advantage, under the French laws of inheritance, of being an only child, so he inherited the whole of his father's and mother's fortunes instead of having to share them equally with brothers and sisters. In the forty-four years from his accession to control of the House until his death, the exports of champagne rose so steeply as to more than double. In 1909, the year before he died, the figure reached 26,000,000 bottles, the highest until 1971. In the same period annual sales of the Krug *marque* increased from 192,021 to 618,260 bottles; meanwhile their wholesale price rose from 2.27 – old – francs to 5.09 francs a bottle.

Yet it would be mistaken to suggest that Paul's path was completely smooth. In some directions he encountered more and more serious problems – through wars, diseases of the vines, troubles with growers and economic recessions – than any of the family until his grandson, the second Paul. They were overcome to a large extent by his ability but, conclusively, because the tide of success for champagne was so strong as to prove irresistible.

Thus he became an extremely rich man; one of the nineteenth-century champagne princes. The textile manufacturers of Reims still regard themselves as the senior mercantile citizens; but they have never known quite such prosperity as that of the great champagne houses about the hinge of the nineteenth and twentieth centuries.

The agreement of the 'new' Krug et Compagnie was drawn up on 14 August 1866, between Hyppolyte de Vivès, the widow Krug – who were each to receive 25 per cent of the profits – and Paul Krug who had 50 per cent, plus an unspecified salary for which he was to devote all his time and attention to the affairs of the company.

It was confined in its 'articles of trade' to the wines of Champagne; and it carried the right to all M. de Vivès' *marques* of the white wines of the region. The capital was fixed at 1,050,000 francs, of which each principal subscribed a third. M. Soullié was to have 4 per cent of the profits before they were divided between the principals.

Joseph I's ambition to direct a champagne house – whenever it was conceived – was not realized until he was forty-three; and even then he had much to do before he could consider himself established. He was at immense pains to bring up his son to occupy that position with complete security. Paul was manoeuvred towards it the more earnestly for being an only child. He went to school first in Reims and then in Paris where, since the French, as realists, regard with horror the English public-school-foster-parent system, he boarded with a family he knew and came home to Reims at weekends. He passed the 'bac' – *baccalauréat* or French academic bachelorship – and was sent to stay in England and Germany to learn those languages. With a German father and an English-born mother he was already a reasonably competent linguist, but his father wanted him to develop beyond competence to fluency, and also to understand the background of his customers. These were the ideal languages for a champagne wine-shipper to know since they covered the main export markets for the wine – apart from Russia – in Britain, the United States of America and Germany. Other European countries, such as Spain, Portugal and Italy, simply were not interested in the commodity.

The single-minded thoroughness that was the keynote to Joseph's character was nowhere more apparent than in the training he planned for his son. He perceived clearly, long before many others who had been longer in the trade, that the relationship between makers and growers was potentially insecure. He may well, too, have foreseen that, as the shippers became more prosperous, the growers – many of whom had barely enough vines to sustain them in a good year and who were desperate in bad years – would not long tolerate that condition. That reinforced his determination to send the young Paul into the vineyards. There he learnt much about viticulture, how to judge grapes and assess their probable development. He also entered into a close relationship with many growers. Often he spent two or three days together in the vines, lodging in the houses of the growers. There he built an understanding which was to stand the firm – and to some extent the growers also – in good stead when the width of the social and financial gap produced the rancour and fundamental division of courses which, so far from being resolved, now pose more, and more acute, problems – for growers, makers and consumers – than ever before.

Above all his father instructed him in tasting and blending. In the seven springs between 1861, when he left school, and 1866, when he inherited the business, the house blended an average of 160,000 bottles of Krug champagne; and, except in 1861 when the American Civil War seriously inhibited exports, over 100,000 bottles for other houses. In establishing the tradition which has endured down to the present, Joseph personally tasted and blended all those wines; and there is no doubt that his son was there with him, under instruction. Certainly, too, he studied closely and learnt much.

As a young man, Paul Krug I was strong and grave-looking; physically heavier and more powerful than his father, facially less like him than his mother, even more like some German ancestor, his features unmistakably Teutonic. Early photographs – posed in the manner of the period and therefore not conclusive – suggest a humourless, unbending man. Others, taken later, show that, whatever may have been the case at first, he grew, with success and an expansive family life, into a relaxed man, cheerful, extrovert and full of an exuberant gaiety.

In 1868 M. de Vivès wrote to him in his invariably courteous fashion to announce his resignation from the firm – 'due to circumstances beyond our control, after twenty years of service which I find have been only too well rewarded by the marks of friendship that have been

Paul Krug I, circa 1865

shown to me.' Joseph Krug, however, would have been delighted by another passage of the letter from one who had been long, and grown wise, in the matters and making of the wine of Champagne. 'I do congratulate you on the success of your wine-making, which has been going well. You cannot complain about your success at New Orleans. Perhaps you should now decide to be a little more generous with your supplies to this fine country, where we must not by our default allow another brand to establish itself.' In that spring – only his second in control of the House – Paul blended 207,048 bottles of Krug; 206,264 bottles for other houses. Indeed, he rapidly won the reputation, in that pragmatic school, of being not only an outstanding blender but one of the most perceptive tasters among the champagne shippers.

His father would, too, have recognized something of his own concern for detail in an announcement the firm issued early in 1870 – 'Having ascertained that the wax round the necks of our champagne bottles was a cause of nuisance to our customers, and being desirous of meeting their wishes, we take pleasure in notifying them that, from and after 1 September 1870, wax will be abandoned and a plain tin capsule bearing the seal of our firm shall be substituted for it to guard against counterfeits.' This was the touch of commercial thoroughness – which some might have thought over-thorough – and integrity – which some might think exaggerated – which, coupled with the essential basis of a good wine, established the standing of the House.

In 1867 Paul wrote to the London vintners, Boord and Son, advising them of the dispatch of some samples of

'Second quality 1864, middling dry and pale: second quality 1865, middling dry but pink. We have added the sample of 1865 as we still have a small lot remaining in hand. We regret that the wine should be so pink; it is a natural colour.'

The demand for the commodity was undoubtedly great, but so was the competition to satisfy it. There probably were more champagne houses in Reims in 1900 than there are now – although the total exports are greater now than then. Some firms flourished and are now bigger than ever. Others failed; they were those who did not establish their reputations sufficiently firmly during the rich years to retain trade in the lean. England was the biggest export market; Krug was primarily an exporting house: therefore England was primarily – and eventually successfully – Paul's target.

Champagne became a symbol in England. It was given the final *imprimatur* of the favour of the Prince of Wales, later Edward VII and incidentally, born within two months of Paul Krug I. To the younger generation the Prince represented gay reaction against the Victorian respectability of his mother, the widow Queen. He was an enthusiastic Francophile and he had a considerable thirst for champagne. His taste was for a dry – really dry – wine. In the nineteenth century, many English champagne drinkers – like sherry drinkers today – liked to order bottles which, though marked 'dry', were actually slightly sweet. The Prince, however, liked a *brut* champagne and his taste eventually moulded the fashion of the sophisticated section of society. When he was out shooting or at the races – especially Ascot – he always had a page standing by with an

adequately chilled bottle of champagne. When the Prince
wanted it he used simply to call 'boy'. As a result it became
almost *de rigueur* in circles near to – or wishing to seem near
to – the Prince, to refer to champagne as 'the Boy'.

On a lower social level where rebellion against
Victorian morality was equally strong, champagne
became the symbol of gay freedom. Joe Saunders, the
factory engineer who had come from the Midlands to earn
a sparse living by singing in East End public houses, was
hardly a fashionable figure. Yet in 1869 Charles Morton,
once the landlord of the Canterbury Music Hall and later
to become the impresario at the Palace Theatre of
Varieties, turned him into an almost legendary figure.
Saunders was physically a fairly handsome man and
Morton gave him the stage name of George Leybourne,
dressed him in top hat, cutaway jacket, topper and cravat
with gloves and silver-topped cane and launched him as
'Champagne Charlie'. Under the influence of success,
Morton elaborated his appearance – Dundreary whiskers,
monocle, striped trousers and a foaming bottle of
champagne took him to the top of the bill in the London
halls. He invited his audience to 'join the boys who make a
noise from now till day is dawning' and created for them a
world of distant romance. Saunders – 'Leybourne' – did
live that life. His engagement fee rose from £25 to £125;
he drove about London in a carriage and pair – or even a
carriage and four – and he drank champagne. The fact that
he drank it with whelks and winkles from street stalls did
not detract from his image. Indeed, it gave Maurice
Willson Disher the unforgettable title *Winkles and
Champagne* for his history of the music hall. Although

Leybourne and his act were known as 'Champagne Charlie', the theme line of his song was 'Moët and Chandon's the wine for me'.

As a consequence of his success, a similar entertainer – Alfred Stevens, the solicitor's clerk turned music hall singer as 'The Great Vance' – was steered into commerccial competition with him – often on the same bill and eventually in simultaneous competition – with 'Clicquot, Clicquot, that's the drink for me'. Apparently this proved effective publicity for those *marques,* since the two continued with 'Cool Burgundy Ben' and 'Sparkling Moselle' but with markedly less success. Champagne was the supreme wine idea in a society where it had become the symbol of splendour. Both 'Leybourne' and 'Vance' made the kind of tragic end – in their forties – that their images demanded. Leybourne, actually sustained by champagne towards the finish, died a few days after he had completed a performance at the Queen's, Poplar, in a state of collapse; while Vance dropped dead on the stage of the Sun at Knightsbridge a few years afterwards. The historian of London theatres, W Macqueen Pope, has argued about Leybourne's 'Champagne Charlie' image that 'those who liked the song best had never tasted champagne and therefore got a tremendous kick out of singing about it.' That might seem likely but, in truth, an item from the Krug history argues to the contrary. In 1889 – having previously labelled their champagne for Threlfalls of Preston – they issued some bottles labelled Champagne Cuvée specially selected for the 'North End' and decorated with a football. There can be no doubt that this referred to Preston North End football club which, in the English

football season of 1888–89, performed the rare 'double' of winning the FA Cup and the Football League in the same season – a performance equalled only once in the following seventy years and only twice since then (though no club has matched that first Preston record of winning the League without losing a match and the Cup without conceding a goal). Few could think of a Lancashire cotton-milling town like Preston as a champagne-drinking place: or that its – or any other British football club's – mass supporters were wine drinkers. There is no more intriguing minor facet of the Krug history than that. Perhaps it was an astute move to exploit a popular and topical event on a national scale – as is often done by publicity-conscious firms nowadays – but it was hardly characteristic of the British wine trade in 1889.

However that may be, it emphasizes the wide popularity of champagne at all levels in England at that time. It was relatively as wealthy a nation as history has known: but the wealth was unevenly distributed. Mayhew's

London Labour and the London Poor and Doré's drawings of the city – probably the finest he ever did – give a poignantly clear picture of the degree, and immense extent, of poverty in Victorian London. At the same time, though, a huge, affluent middle class grew up almost overnight.

Hitherto wine had been largely the privilege of the upper class in Britain. Now, suddenly, it was within the reach of hundreds of times as many people. In 1851 – the year of the Great Exhibition – Mrs Beeton suggests that a family income of £1,000 – frequent in that society – justified a domestic staff of a cook, two housemaids and a manservant. The household budget could allocate about £2 a week for drink, including entertainment. At that time the retail price of champagne in London was between £2 18s and – for the finest – £4 4s a dozen. Even as late as 1860 the dearest wine of the region on a London merchant's list was 'Choice Rare Sillery *sec (non mousseux)*' at £4 4s a dozen; while Moët et Chandon 1st growth 1846, Perrier Jouet 1st growth, Mumm 1st growth, Giesler and 'Mme Clicquot's *à la Russe*' were all £3; and 'The celebrated Epernay 1848 vintage', £2 the dozen case. In 1880 all shippers increased their prices – most by four to eight shillings a dozen, but Krug by only three – after the bad vintages of 1876, 1877 and – the smallest of the century at barely two million gallons – 1879. Yet, even then, the highest price asked by a firm of London importers was £3 12s a dozen – for Perrier Jouet, Pfungst, or Ruinart – while Bollinger was £3 5s, Mumm et Piper £3 8s, Krug £3 3s, and £3 5s.

In the opulent London of the clubs, theatres and

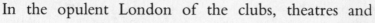

NORTH-END

restaurants, the countless service messes, the universities, all the resorts of the British middle and upper classes, champagne was consumed on such a prodigal scale that the export figures doubled in twenty-five years from the death of Joseph Krug I to 1891.

From 1871, and the end of the Franco-Prussian War until 1914 Champagne enjoyed a period of unbroken peace and – apart from the financial crisis of 1876 – prosperity such as it had never known before. It seemed as if world demand for its wine would never stop increasing. During the 1870s the champagne industry became something akin to an empire. The senior representatives of the great houses travelled through the Americas, the Russias, Germany, Britain and northern Europe like plenipotentiaries, talking in the financially weighty language of ultimate luxury. They were often not concerned with specific sales: that matter could be conducted by local agents; but to re-establish existing relations among the higher echelons of their customers. More valuably, they might establish their name and standing in a fresh and influential quarter. It is tempting to quote Shakespeare out of context and describe them as 'seeking the bubble reputation'.

This was the centre of Paul Krug's aim. He probably was fortunate in having – through his English-born mother and the visits to England organized by his father – a far better understanding than most Frenchmen of the people who were his ultimate customers. The British attitude to wine is unusual, if not unique. They are not wine-producers nor, in character, wine-drinkers – like the Germans they are a nation of beer drinkers. The minority

Paul Krug I. England, 1887

of British people who drink wine – and, despite the recent increase in wine consumption, they are still a minority – have an attitude towards wine which is often incomprehensible to the people who live in countries which make it, and who drink it by nature. To the Frenchman, Italian or Spaniard of any social stratum, wine is not even a necessity, it is an automatic concomitant of being a living human being. When the British drink wine they do so consciously, not naturally like the Latin races. Unlike the born wine drinkers they rarely simply accept it, because it is not simple to them – nor natural. Thus they tend to be more critical, more demanding, almost certainly less informed, perhaps affectedly ignorant. The wine-snob is all but invariably an English or American phenomenon. So is the 'wine is all nonsense' attitude. Frenchmen drink more wine than anyone in England, but most of them drink the produce of the same vineyard or vineyard-village all their lives. The British, on the other hand, have long had the wines of the world available no further away than the off-licences in the main street of the nearest town or village. In how many towns in France, even now, could one buy the wines of all the French regions, Spain, Portugal, Italy, Yugoslavia, Austria, Hungary – and, probably Algeria, Morocco, Greece, Chile – as British people can in at least 4,000 shops? A wide choice of wines has been available from British wine merchants for more than a century. So, unlike the people of the wine countries, the Briton has no loyalty, neither does he find it convenient always to drink any specific local, regional or even national wine. He would think it reasonable, if he could afford it, to take an Italian vermouth – perhaps with a Dutch gin – as an apéritif; Spanish sherry with his soup; a German hock with his fish; a French claret or Burgundy with the meat; and port – from Portugal – with his cheese. Because nineteenth-century England was the most economically powerful nation in the world and the centre of a vast *entrepôt* trade, all these wines were, and still are, available throughout the country. Such a catholic palate, offered a wide range, may favour one particular kind of wine – sherry, claret, hock or port – but, granted an approximately even level of quality, the choice as to what type, brand or label of that kind of wine is often likely to be subjective.

Given the circumstances of the time, the fashion for champagne was predictable. It was a relative novelty, visually exciting, lively to taste and highly stimulating to drink. The Prince of Wales established it as the fashion and his influence prevailed not only in England but in France also. His preference for dry champagne, however, cut across the home trade. In France which is, after all, its country of origin, the taste was for a sweet wine, generally to be drunk at dessert, and, on the popular level, that is still often the case there. That suited many of the shippers because the addition of sugar to a wine often serves to conceal flaws which would be painfully apparent if it were unsugared and dry. For that reason the idealists among the champagne shippers might say that the '*brut*' palate proved beneficial to the standards of the wine.

Thus, for the third time, the power of the British imperial purse changed the character of a wine from the palate of the country which made it. The first instance was that of port, when British wine shippers sought to exploit the fiscal advantages of trade with Portugal. Normally the natural red wine of the country would have matured to a full, dry flavour. Under British direction it was turned into a sweet, fortified dessert wine by a process which arrests fermentation through the addition of brandy before all the sugar has fermented into alcohol. The result is a unique, but an English – not a Portuguese – wine. It could never be the native drink of people who live under the sun of the latitude of Portugal.

The second case was of sherry when, to meet the demands of the British market, the splendidly dry wine of Spain was caramellized into a sugary dessert confection for ladies to take with a slice of cake in the morning or at mid-afternoon. Those were concessions to the adolescent, senile or simply naïve sweet tooth of the British. The call for dry champagne as opposed to the sweet of the other markets was more sophisticated but perhaps even more subjective. Despite the claims of other importers, and the point-blank refusal of one shipper to supply a *brut*, it was enforced by British purchasing power. Once the fashion for dry champagne had been set in the biggest export market, competition between the exporters resolved itself into a series of bids for the fashion within the fashion – the favoured *marque* of dry champagne.

The British wine market has always been swayed by fashion – which may, nowadays, be no more than advertisement-saturation. It is apparent in modern Britain

in the consumption of the widely-publicised Bristol
Cream, EMVA Cream, Mateus Rosé, Blue Nun, Mouton
Cadet, Hirondelle. The same applies in France to the public
for patent *apéritifs* and whiskies – but not for wine. The
British were open to persuasion – and some of it had been
going on for a long time.

Krug, from the very youth of the House, could hardly
lead that particular field in the 1870s. The Prince of Wales
was an eclectic drinker but his conversion to *brut*
champagne is attributed to drinking the 1865 Ayala 'Very
Dry' at the Bullingdon Club during his brief and
interrupted period as an undergraduate at Oxford. It has
been noted, too, that the champagnes featured in the two
popular music hall songs were Clicquot and Moët et
Chandon; while according to Christie's auction records,
the most esteemed and costly *marque* through the 1870s and
'80s was Pommery et Greno.

During the 1870s Paul Krug I continued to make good
champagne – much of it for other people. In 1879 he
blended twice as much for other shippers as his own
163,321 bottles. He was labelling Krug for the Cunard
Line; the Panama Railway; the Central America Steam
Ship Line; Smith Bros and Co of New Orleans;
Emmanuel Nataris of Alexandria; Simon y Cie of
Buenos Aires; Elorze Lejarany Cie of Mazatlyan; Quellyn
Roberts and Co – still in business in Chester; S Slojarovits
Bralia, Roumania; A C Mitchell-Innes of Grants Lane,
Calcutta; the Garrison Club, Quebec; the Bachelors Club:
and Reynell and Co, Yokohama and Haogo.

He was highly conscious – and proud – of its quality. In a
letter of 1869 to Inglis who was then responsible for his

London sales, he wrote 'Now the stock of 1865 is exhausted and nothing can be done to renew it' and then, in a characteristic Krug phrase – 'as similar wine and quality are not to be found in the Champagne country.'

Sales of Krug in England grew steadily but, if the *marque* had not made the progress Paul wanted, he felt that was because it was not being presented in the right way – or more probably, not in the right quarter. It was a question of prestige. He aspired to a single label which said simply 'Krug': and he was near to achieving that ambition. In 1880 Colonel Fred Campbell, a former Artillery officer, found that 'Gunner's pay would not go round' and, like many a well brought-up young Briton with no particular professional qualifications before and since, entered the London wine trade. Within a couple of years a series of amalgamations found him one of the partners in the firm of City wine-shippers and agents called Reid, Pye, Cunningham and Campbell. In the course of years they were to lose their Cunningham; acquire and lose a Hall; be bombed out of the City and move to the West End where they are now Reid, Pye and Campbell of Jermyn Street.

In 1883 they became Krug's British agents. For years an apocryphal story about that agency has passed round wine trade circles linked with Colonel Campbell, who was to become a major figure in the trade but was then only a junior partner in the firm. Nevertheless, according to legend, as soon as the first supply of the fine vintage Krug of 1875 arrived, the Colonel decided to submit it to the judgement of the two firms he considered most effective in selling champagne. They were Berry Bros and Rudd of St James's, whom he thought the most influential West End merchants; and W H Bauly, the leading champagne specialists among the City marketing houses, with an extensive network of contacts through the retail trade both in London and the provinces. Accordingly he invited Henry Berry, the senior partner of Berry Bros and Rudd and W E Bauly to lunch and gave them Krug with the meal. As they sat over their port afterwards, Bauly took out his cheque book and said simply 'How much is it? I will take the entire consignment.' 'But', said Berry, 'I want it all – what is the price?' The story ends with each having half the shipment. Although the entire circumstances are fictitious, they paraphrase the fact that a number of eminent merchants – though Berry Bros were not among them – did, at various times offer to buy an entire British allocation of Krug. It also compresses the British aspect of the firm's history between 1875 and 1885, when it won the entrée to that uniquely English society where a family or social connection is more influential than money, and a nod is better than a wink. From that point its quality ensured its acceptance in the specific sector of the particular market where recognition is most prestigious and, both directly and indirectly, most financially rewarding. It emphasizes, too, the service which, for almost a hundred years, Reid, Pye and Campbell rendered Krug in a world that began to die with the outbreak of the First World War.

Krug first appeared in that infallible yardstick of British estimation, a Christie's catalogue, in 1886 at the disposal of a wine merchant's stock, when lots of their *Crémant* made 95s to 103s a dozen. In 1887, the extremely fine 1868 vintage went for 92s a dozen.

Another Christie's auction – of March 1888 – affords a most revealing view of wine tastes and fashions of the time. The Krug *Private Cuvée* 1874 fetched 100s a dozen, while the château-bottled Lafite of the same year – and that was as outstanding a vintage for claret as it was for champagne – went for 56s to 58s. However, in the same sale, the Pommery et Greno 1874 *Extra Sec* made 180s to 190s. In May 1889 the 'Krug 1880–1881 *Private Cuvée Extra Sec* landed 1885' made 72s. Nothing more sharply defines the relative esteem in which commodities are held than the sale of similar items in a single auction. At Christie's in July 1891 four outstanding wines of great vintages were sold. The price for the claret – Château Mouton Rothschild 1870, no less – was 40s to 45s; for the port – Croft 1870, bottled 1873 – 63s to 65s; for the burgundy – the fine Romanée-Conti 1874 – 64s to 84s; meanwhile, the Krug *Private Cuvée* 1880 made 112s to 115s. It is illuminating of the standing not only of Krug, but of all champagne in the 1890s – a period which found an affinity too with that particular wine. Paul Krug I had made his *marque*.

8

The dominion of Paul I

The first Paul Krug inherited a comfortable security which he turned into quite immense wealth and influence. London was only one of many triumphs, albeit a major and significant one, for Paul I. Within a few years there was a fundamental assumption of power in Reims.

In 1898 477,676 bottles were sold from the Krug cellars; in 1900, 503,452 bottles; in 1902, 521,963 bottles; in 1903, 626,711 bottles. They included the outstanding vintages of 1892, 1893, 1895, 1896 and 1897. Meanwhile, the equally fine 1899 and 1900 were maturing in the cellars.

At this time the firm paid Paul Krug I a salary of 2,000,000 francs a year. 'Not,' his grandson remarked drily 'two million francs printed in tens on paper, but gold francs,' adding, almost as an afterthought, 'and there was no tax then.' This was a wealth beyond his father's imagination. He lived a life to match, in a large house with many servants. In Normandy he had a holiday house and two farms – one for stock and one for dairy: he built a Protestant church for the congregation in Reims; and, in

1909, he and his wife sent their children friendly notes to tell them they were making each of them a gift of 100,000 francs.

All that lay in the realm of remote possibility early in 1868 when a letter from de Vivès congratulated him on 'your satisfaction with your journey to Normandy'. Later in the same year he married Caroline Harlé who lived in Rouen and, for the rest of their lives, Normandy became a second home for the couple and their children. Bénouville was their holiday house near the sea and, in due course, Paul farmed there.

Bénouville, the west side

The weather and the vintages were kind to him during his early years in charge. Wine of four fine years – 1861, 1862, 1863 and 1865 – remained from his father's day as a reassuring support against a bad summer. Then, immediately after he inherited, 1867 was good; 1868 outstanding; 1869 indifferent; 1870 excellent. He was too good a blender to neglect such opportunities. He produced 330,384 bottles under the Krug *marque* in 1870; 427,678 bottles in 1872. Profits were held comfortably above 300,000 francs and rose to 475,000 francs in 1872 – a reassuring figure in the year after the Franco-Prussian War.

He took sufficient confidence from it to set up a fresh establishment of home, cellars and offices. He bought a generous plot in a good situation on the north of the city, inside the railway and conveniently near the goods depot. It was almost triangular, with a frontage on to the wide Boulevard Lundy, making a corner with Rue Coquebert and backed by the Rue de la Justice. The nearest neighbours were Roederer and Irroy.

The complex of offices, warehouse, loading bays and cellars was set about a generous yard with a gate giving on to Rue Coquebert. From the gateway the offices and loading bay lie to the right; ahead, the pediment – inset with a clock and now bearing a vari-coloured covering of Virginia creeper – and the cellars; fermenting barrels and stores on the left.

Facing west on to the boulevard he built No 40 Boulevard Lundy, known in the family as '*le Quarante*'. A massive house with a turretted Mansard roof, it was large enough to accommodate Paul, his wife, their ten children and a formidable domestic staff. There was an extensive garden between the house and the cellars, domestic quarters were built into the outer walls and a *logis* within the deep archway giving from the garden on to the corner of the boulevard with Rue Coquebert. The extensive cellars ran to the full extent under the garden and *'le Quarante'*. The yard allowed plenty of space for the manoeuvres of the long drays, drawn by pairs of proudly massive Percherons which rumbled thunderously across the stones of the yard and the cobbles of the boulevard : and it can comfortably accommodate the huge lorries of 1976.

No 40 Boulevard Lundy, however, had no place in modern times as a family house. Imposing and expansive, it was built with a nineteenth-century disregard for cost and could only be maintained in a society equipped with an inexhaustible reservoir of low-paid domestic labour. In 1971 it was demolished and replaced by a block of flats – though the cellars still run beneath them. The three families of the present-day – of Paul II, Henri and Rémi – live in the houses within the walls; while the self-contained, three-roomed *logis* is set aside for visitors.

'Le Quarante', however, remains a place of family tradition; a whole group of legends was created around the father, mother and ten children who lived and grew up there. The completely dominant head of the household was Paul I; father-figure, success-symbol, increasingly expansive with growing success. He retained his father's perfectionism in a more open-handed way – 'Never cut coins in four' was his maxim. He became a larger-than-life figure within the family because, having inherited a fortune and vastly increased it, he enjoyed it to the full. Immensely active, he attended to business in a flurry of activity – early

Le Quarante

morning office work if the day proffered outside interest, entertainment, a fine meal, *la chasse*. All his life, too, he was an indefatigable letter writer. Even when he went on holiday to Normandy he took the letter book with him. As a result the indelible copies of his correspondence – business and personal – fill several shelves of one of the many and large rooms he built so prodigally into the complex which was – and mostly still is – the Krug establishment.

In 1876 the kindly, polite Hyppolyte de Vivès died and, in due course, Paul bought up his interest in the firm.

Paul Krug I was a man of immense vitality and gusto: he loved hunting, shooting, and riding. He smoked large cigars; enjoyed claret – which he bought by the barrel and had bottled in Reims – often in champagne bottles – madeira and brandy. He produced and raised a family with characteristic generosity. His wife, the former Caroline Harlé, was hardly likely to do more than live in the formidable shadow. She was the practical woman who ran a huge household, brought up ten children and enjoyed her husband. The ten brothers and sisters remain a kind of mythology within the family: the sensitive Joseph II was to become the head of the household: Emma, lived to be 101 despite breaking a leg at ninety-six and an arm at 100: she and Louisa, who had twelve children, married two Seydoux brothers. Henri was killed in the First World War, serving in the Alpine forces; Jacques, the clergyman, strained the congregation by the length of his speech at the wedding of Paul II; Emile, the never-caught but firmly identified black sheep of the family, inexplicably travelled the country with a free cinema show. Alice, a military nurse and a spinster, said by the family to have 'married the army', inherited her father's vitality and, at the age of eighty-eight in 1975, was relished and admired by nephews and nieces and their children for her wit. Charlotte, at ninety-four, set off to see Afghanistan. Henriette married Emile Daeschner, the diplomat who, early in his career was an attaché in the embassy in London and went on, through a series of European appointments to end his career as French ambassador in Washington. Maggie, twenty years younger than Joseph, married Adolphe Jacquesson's grandson. Alice recalls the German governesses who used to set the girls of the family to scrape the floor-polish from between the floorboards with needles. Life in the household at *le Quarante,* though, was by no means always like that; photographs taken on the beach in Normandy are period pieces of a warm, relaxed family.

Paul I's embrace was wider than his family: he made friends easily, and commanded loyalty. He was a member

Paul Krug I with his children, 1891
BACK ROW: *Henriette, Jacques, Emma, Joseph II, Louisa*
MIDDLE ROW: *Emile, Caroline, Paul I, Charlotte*
FRONT ROW: *Maggie, Alice*

of the *Cercle de Reims* – the main club of the town where the champagne shippers met, ate, played cards and talked 'shop'. Chiefly, however, he liked to shoot – especially the wild boar of the Montagne. He used often to take with him his shipping clerk, Hermann Koch, another in the firm's line of German and Swiss clerks. M. Koch was a lively-minded bachelor, a collector of furniture and china with no family except the spinster sister who kept house for him. On one shooting excursion, when he went into a butcher's shop to buy some *charcuterie* for lunch he saw the butcher chopping up the carcase of a boar on – appropriately but surprisingly – a splendid eighteenth-century, marble-topped, inlaid, kingwood *table de gibier* (hunting lodge table). He at once commiserated with the butcher on having to do such exacting work on such an unsuitable working surface. He would, he insisted, bring him a proper table. Within a few days he returned with a sturdy butcher's block, made in the Krug workshop. The butcher accepted it with delight; M. Koch took away the *table de gibier* and both were more than satisfied. Hermann Koch worked from youth until his death for the House of Krug. When, subsequently, his sister died it was found that, having no known relations, they had left their possessions to the Krug family, who had provided them with contented security all their adult lives. The legacy included not only the *table de gibier* but an usually fine collection of eighteenth-century Jacquots and Jacquelines. They are the pottery figure mugs – similar to English toby jugs – which were used as drinking vessels in northern France and Belgium. They are now, also like toby jugs, rare antiques, particularly the decorative types made for

regimental messes which Herman Koch specially collected.

Another faithful of the firm was M. Payen, *chef de cave,*
who worked in the Krug cellars for fifty years; he had
three wives – married the third at seventy-two – and
seventeen children. Paul, who never failed to blend every
one of the House's wines, often called him in for an
opinion on the final *mélange*, but he had no decision in the
matter. Sometimes, too, an old friend from Le Mesnil
would be invited to taste it. He was M. Launois, an
enthusiastic amateur of wine who, when he went to take
the waters at Contrexeville, always took a supply of
champagne with him.

Having weathered the two years of the Franco-Prussian
War and subsequent occupation, the firm never had a
genuinely bad time – apart from the commercial crisis of
1876 – in the forty-four years of Paul I's control. Of the

Paul Krug I and Monsieur Koch

same age, within a few weeks, as the Prince of Wales, he was in tune with the times and their tastes and he easily kept pace with the champagne boom. He put out an *'Extra Sec'* in 1874 and 1884; *'Extra Dry'* in 1880. In 1880 he priced his *Private Cuvée* at 6s 0d a bottle; while in 1891, he announced that 'the *Private Cuvée* will be of a drier type and the price will be increased by 5s 0d a case, owing to the scarcity of high-class wines.'

There were setbacks, both internally and in the wider prospect. A shipping clerk's coolly factual – yet none the less harrowing – record of shipwrecks of the *Electric Spark*, the *Georges* and the *Visir* in the Atlantic gales of November 1869 accounts for the loss of some 4,000 cases of champagne.

An illuminating aspect of the feeling and fellowship between members of the nineteenth-century champagne aristocracy is the story of Henri Lanson and the Krug '87. The Krugs and the Lansons have been intimates for a century. At a time when Paul I was making his major advance in the British market Henri Lanson came to him with a proposition. He was, he said, not content with his 1887 vintage. Had Paul Krug a good wine of that year and, if so, would he sell him some? Paul Krug had a satisfactory wine. For what market, he asked, did Henri Lanson want it? 'For England' was the answer. Today that would have been enough to produce something more than mere refusal. Paul Krug sold Henri Lanson an extremely large parcel of his 1887, which underwent *remuage* and *dégorgement* in the Lanson cellars and then, bearing the Lanson label, was sent to England. Agents are agents and customers are customers – the fact remains that the Krug

'87 under the label sold well; the Krug '87 bearing the Lanson label did not. Henri Lanson, downcast, discussed the matter with Paul Krug, who offered to buy back all that remained. It was shaken and disgorged in the Krug cellars and sent to Britain where it sold completely successfully. Whether there is a moral in this or not, it should endure as one of the more salutary of wine stories.

One of the salient characteristics of the Krug family is loyalty. They rarely criticize any of their members, least of all Paul I. On one issue, however, they at least 'regret' a decision of his which may have made a major difference in the firm's fortunes. In 1888 he bought twenty hectares (fifty acres) of vineyards – by Champagne, or indeed, any French standards, a huge holding – in several parcels on the south of the village of Mailly. This was – and is – some of the best vineland in Champagne. The growers of Mailly, in effect, went on strike against the shippers who challenged their prices during the inter-war slump. In consequence they built and established their own co-operative and, ever since, the extremely desirable, 100 per cent wine of Mailly has been in short supply to shippers. Paul I sold the land in 1904 – 'to pay for my wedding' his son Joseph used later to say, jokingly. It was, though, no joke for his successors.

The heaviest affliction in the history of viticulture was, of course, phylloxera, the louse which, between 1870 and 1920 killed off most of the fine vines of Europe. It came from America and the only vines resistant to it are American. So, after experiments of all kinds – spraying, flooding and directing carbon disulphide gas on to the roots – it was recognized that the only means of preserving

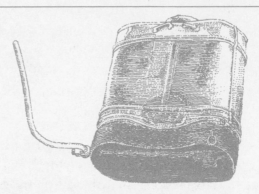

the culture of wine grapes in Europe was by grafting them on to American roots. This has now been done virtually all over the world, but early progress was damagingly slow. It was hindered at first by sheer lack of knowledge. The *Champenois* scientist, H E Manceau, was among the early researchers into the blight. Secondly, there was skimping of funds to fight the danger; too many people did not perceive that the alternatives were heavy work, blank years and high expenditure on the one hand; complete destruction of the vineyards of Europe on the other. Finally the clearing process was delayed by the unthinking opposition of the small growers. In Champagne a group of shippers provided the finance to buy phylloxera-resistant stock and direct the grafting. Even that move, however, could not overcome the handicap imposed on anti-phylloxera measures within almost all the vineyards throughout Europe – peasant stupidity, suspicion and stubborn refusal to be inspected or directed. Fortunately for Champagne, the louse found its chillier climate less congenial than that of the more southerly vineyards, and it came as far north as the Marne much later and with slightly less damaging effect than elsewhere in France. It attacked

Bordeaux and Portugal in 1869 and spread relatively rapidly through the Beaujolais, the Rhône and Burgundy by 1878. For a decade it seemed that it was completely repelled by the cold of Champagne, but in 1890 it arrived. Moët et Chandon bought the first affected vineyards and burnt every twig of growth on them.

This was said to be the first time the method of complete destruction – the method employed in Switzerland – had been used in France. Unfortunately subsequent steps were less prompt and definite. In July 1891 a control syndicate was formed to deal with the problem. Recognizing the need for urgency it began to act – having diseased vines eradicated and paying compensation – before an executive committee had been elected. In August, when elections for the committee were held, the voters were offered two lists of candidates – one nominated by growers, the other by the local authority – either to be elected *en bloc*. The second contained members of the Champagne Chamber of Commerce which was regarded by the growers as a shippers' organisation and, accordingly, they voted in their own candidates. The *Préfet*, frustrated in his well-intentioned but bureaucratic purpose, first procrastinated and then co-opted twenty-seven members – mostly from the Chamber of Commerce – whereupon the growers' representatives resigned. Resistance to the replanters went to the point of violence and, as happened in so many vineyards of France, while people quarrelled, the louse continued its deadly incursion.

The plague took firm hold and, by 1910, a third of the Champagne vineyards had been destroyed. Yet, even though carbon disulphide was available to them free, 8,000 out of 25,000 growers refused to use it; and even when the American stock was offered to them at no charge until their vines were cropping again, more than half of them rejected the offer. The restocking was interrupted by the First World War and was not completed until the 1920s. Yet, somehow, a steady output was maintained.

The obstruction of the growers had origins fiercer than the peasant's instinctive mistrust of the world outside his own. The international demand for champagne had made the shippers rich beyond even their reasonable hopes. The growers had enjoyed no comparable prosperity. Those who produced indifferent grapes could be, and were, ignored by the great houses. Those who grew the best had still, in some cases, to accept an unreasonably low price set by a shipper who could always go elsewhere without faring substantially less well in terms of quality. There were enlightened shippers who, from altruism or because they saw the potential dangers, did not exploit this situation; but others did; and some went far beyond those bounds.

Already, in 1884 Paul Krug, whose ear was close to the ground among the vines, and a number of other influential growers, had pressed the foundation of the *Syndicat du Commerce des Vins de Champagne.* This body, not to be confused with the subsequent and similarly orientated *Syndicat General des Vignerons,* was a grouping of shippers concerned to establish mutual interest with the growers. It contributed substantially towards dealing with phylloxera in the *vignoble* but it did not succeed in its ultimate aim because there was more at issue than price-rates between honest growers and honest shippers.

In 1891, Napoleon Legrand who described himself as 'Secretary-archivist to the Syndicate for the Champagne Wine Trade' published, in an edition of only fifty copies – all printed on Japan paper – a book entitled *Champagne*. It had much to say that was wise and perceptive: and one passage looked prophetically to future issues – 'A few manufacturers have settled in the centres of our trade who produce sparkling wine with wine inferior in both quality and price which is grown in other districts. Those engaged in this new industry have no scruples about selling those delusive "Champagne" (cork-blowers) under the counterfeit name of Champagne wine.'

If that was true – and there is little doubt that it was – the matter was not even so simple as that of oppressive price-fixing. It meant that the grapes of growers in Champagne were being ignored while cheaper fruit from other regions was being used to produce wine which was to be sold falsely under the name of champagne.

In 1904 Paul Krug I and the Marquis Bertrand de Mun, head of Clicquot, were among the founders of a *Syndicat* designed specifically to protect the grower from exploitation. Even a majority of men of goodwill, however, could not control the activities of those who saw the prospect of quick, large and dishonest profits from a market which would buy anything in what appeared to be a champagne bottle.

That safeguard could be applied only by the government; and the government was conspicuously reluctant to take any meaningful action. Eventually, in 1908, it defined the legal limits of the *Champagne viticole*, specifically excluding the vineyards of Aube, but including some of

Aisne. Without doubt the aggrieved growers of the Marne believed the 'foreign' wine was being brought from, or through, Aube – probably both.

Paul Krug I had long anticipated – in essence if not in detail – but did not live to see, the event which ensured that none of his descendants would ever know quite such an empire as he had enjoyed. On the evidence of strict timing, the government's procrastination precipitated the Ay Riots. It can be argued that the rift between the growers and shippers was by then so sharp and so fundamental that such an explosion of resentment was inevitable, whatever the government might have done. On the other hand, the rioters – whose declared purpose was to wreck the cellars of the firms that had used 'foreign' grapes to make 'champagne' – left the Bollinger establishment – which had certainly not transgressed – completely untouched. There was, though, a certain lack of discrimination, and some other houses which were also blameless were nevertheless attacked.

The trouble escalated gradually. After the *vignerons* held meetings at Damery and Epernay in 1910 they raided consignments of 'foreign' wines at Epernay, Hautvillers and Damery. A law of 11 February 1911 provided for close inspection and severe punishment for the *'fraudeurs'*; and again excluded the Aube vineyards. Now there were demonstrations in Aube and, in April, a vacillating government gave way once more and, in yet another bill, repealed the previous limits.

That news reached the vineyards of the Marne in the evening of 11 April 1911 and that night a savage mob rioted, wrecked shippers' premises at Damery – the central point of their resentment – Dizy and Ay.

It was said that almost five thousand growers swarmed into the little town of Ay. Dragoons were sent in to quell the disturbance but they stood by inactive while the mob, having wrecked cellars, smashed casks and bottles until the streets ran with wine, then turned their attention to the houses of the growers they believed guilty. There is no doubt that the government was profoundly shocked by the violence of the *Champenois* reaction. They suppressed it by sending some 40,000 troops – 'More soldiers than Winegrowers in Champagne' said the headline in *l'Humanité* – but they did legislate to protect the growers.

Even then the law contained flaws which invited trouble. In the first place it created two classes of champagne; one from the better vineyards of the Marne and Aisne; the other – to be called *Champagne Deuxième Zone* – from the few excluded vineyards of the Marne and those of Aube, Wassy and Seine-et-Marne. In addition, while sparkling wines from other parts of France were to be called *mousseux*, a shipper within Champagne could make champagne from local grapes and *mousseux* from imported grapes, provided the two cellars were separated by the width of a street. It was law which tried to please essentially conflicting groups; and, like all legislation of that kind, it proved impracticable.

It was not all the *vignerons* had asked for but, although they pressed for more, they saw it as something gained. The official excise figures – by showing that more 'champagne' was sold than Champagne *viticole* produced – proved that the growers' accusations were justified. In the event it was over two years before the bill was ratified. The growers were promised another and fairer law, but the 1914 war broke out before it could be framed. It was not finally passed until 1927 and it still applies. It allows only one classification of champagne: and it admits the vineyards of Aube.

The year 1909 brought Paul Krug I yet more success. He sold 618,260 bottles of champagne under his own label – most of them of the distinguished 1900 and 1904 vintages; and, at the Seattle Exposition, Krug took the Grand Prix from all the other *grandes marques* for an exhibit of champagne. That was, too, the high peak of the age of champagne; the point for a triumphal exit.

Paul Krug died in 1910, as he had been born, within weeks of that Prince of Wales who confirmed the fashion for champagne, became King Edward VII of England, and drank Krug.

Paul Krug I, in old age

Joseph II and Madame Krug

The Krugs do not run to type. Joseph II was his father's son in affection and loyalty, but little in other ways. His appearance gave none of his father's impression of power; when he joined a hunting party he took a camera with him instead of a gun; and he did not want to be the head of a champagne house. Indeed, it is probable that he became one only out of kindness – to please his father.

He was brought up close to the business, had an instinctively sensitive – and well practised – palate and the family aptitude for blending: but he did not want to stay in Reims. He travelled much in the East – to India, China, Indo-China, Japan and Australia – and at twenty-four he joined the Army. Seven years later he left the military service with the rank of captain, and declared his ambition to become a sailor. Before that could happen the family, his loyalty and filial conscience persuaded him to enter the firm and, by 1903, he was running it jointly with his father.

When he inherited control of the House in 1910 he was forty-one years old; the business was well established; and,

Joseph Krug II, 1910

over his first four years, Krug sales of their own *marque*
averaged 480,000 bottles for 2,400,000 francs. He was not
at heart a competitor like his father or his grandfather. It
was said that he was 'too nice to be in business', that he was
'too kind' and 'would believe anybody'. He was, though,
right for Krug in his time; the *marque* stood in high esteem;
the House could sell all it produced; and, valuably, he was
good at tasting and blending, technically sound and
sympathetic in his handling of staff. His tact, consideration
and sheer lack of aggression or self-interest were probably
more valuable to his firm than greater strength or
acquisitiveness was likely to have proved in face of the
prevailing mood of the growers.

A jolly, humorous, kindly man, fond of children –
whom he teased without grieving – he had an immense

feeling for his family who knew him, happily, as 'Uncle Joe'.

In 1904, when he was thirty-four, he married Jeanne Hollier Larousse. Eleven years younger than her husband, she was the great niece of Pierre Larousse, the lexicographer who compiled the towering, fifteen-volume *Grand Dictionnaire Universel du XIXe Siècle*; and founded the publishing house renowned for its authoritative reference books. Jeanne Larousse had inherited a similar quality of encyclopaedic mind, and had with it a sense of humour which, in its different way, complemented her husband's. The Larousses, she would say, 'are interested in anything – so long as it is spelt properly.' Her arguments – debates as distinct from quarrels – with her brother Pierre on his visits to Reims were famous within the family and their friends as outstanding entertainment. Jeanne, according to family tradition, 'was always right.'

Joseph Krug II with his wife, Jeanne

In 1912 their only child, Paul II was born. Both he and his sons hold the couple in an unmistakeably loving respect which goes far beyond family piety. Joseph II, though, did not long enjoy his inheritance and family life before the First World War broke out. He was at once called back to his artillery unit. Only half the vintage of 1914 was gathered. Although the grapes were good, most of the men who might have gathered them were already at war; and some of the vineyards of the Marne were within range of German guns: at least thirty and perhaps more of the *vendangeurs* were killed. Even those who were out of range were so close to the front line that no kind of transport or telephone service was available; there was a shortage of casks; the growers did not know whether to pick; the shippers did not know whether to buy – or whether, if they did, they would merely be making wine for the Germans. Meanwhile, some hundreds of thousands of bottles of disgorged Krug champagne – ripe for German drinking if they were left there – were moved from Reims to Châlons. As Châlons came under the threat of occupation, the whole stock was moved again to Paris. There it was stored in the cellars underneath the Seydoux family textile agency in the Rue de Paradis, where it remained until the end of the war, when it returned to Reims as an eminently marketable commodity.

Madame Krug conducted the affairs of the champagne house. She herself blended the 1915 vintage. It was unique for a Krug; dark, not far short of rosé, because she had to make the entire *cuvée* from black grapes since, in war conditions, no transport was available to bring white from the Côte des Blancs. It is a deep, rich wine and Ian Maxwell

Campbell relates how a champagne expert – Colonel Sarson – who did not usually favour Krug, was extremely enthusiastic about Mme Krug's *cuvée*.

In 1915 Joseph was wounded and taken prisoner during the fierce fighting in the Ardennes where he was, in truth, defending his home. After attempting to escape, he was in close confinement when a letter from his wife told him that she was making a *cuvée*. How, he asked, when he next wrote, had she contrived to buy the grapes? Years afterwards he used humourously to vow his imprisonment worried him less than the news that they had been bought on a loan from a Paris bank. In the event, the vintage sold out completely; Reid, Pye and Campbell disposed of the British allocation in the shortest possible time.

Phylloxera, added to bombardment, trench warfare and shortage of labour, reduced wine to minor stature against the background of war. Mme Krug, with the assistance of the redoubtable cellar-master, M. Payen, managed to keep the business moving. After the shock of 1914, 1915 and 1916 were remarkably successful years for a city so near the firing line, with 323,850 and 311,497 bottles respectively. That standard could not be maintained; in 1917 the figure was no more than 172,411 bottles; and in 1918, 98,219 bottles was the lowest since 1858.

Apart from the business, Mme Krug concerned herself increasingly with nursing in the local hospital; and she maintained a dispensary – and later a hospital – in the cellars at Rue Coquebert. Photographs in the family albums show vividly the kind of underground life lived in the firm's cellars during the days which added up to almost three years of German artillery bombardment. Shell fire was deliberately aimed at the cathedral which the Germans insisted was being used as a look-out tower, and as a result the glorious Rose Window was shattered and a huge fire started in the nave.

To a greater degree even than in London during the blitz of the later war, the city's life went underground. The cellars were proof against shell fire and many of the Krug staff lived down there for weeks on end. Food, water supplies and sanitation were adequate and people not only worked, ate and drank down there, but school classes, church services, parties and concerts were held. Passages were cut through the chalk to connect the cellars of the great houses, which were used also to house reserve troops and their munitions on a vast scale. It is said that not a single bottle of champagne in the cellars was so much as cracked by the German bombardment – but by no means all were proof against the thirst of the troops who devised some extremely ingenious methods of tapping them or smuggling them out.

Photographs of the time show the improvised cooking stoves, crates and packing cases converted into chairs and beds by layers of blankets; but at the same time there are silver candlesticks on the scrupulously polished dining table and sideboard; while a sewing-machine emphasizes the domesticity of the scene.

When the bombardment reached its peak, all but a few of the citizens left. Mme Krug and Mme Goulden, wife of another Reims champagne shipper, who together ran a hospital, were the last two women left in Reims. Mme Krug was twice gassed – with the gas known as Yperite which attacks the throat and eyes. Eventually, in 1917, the

Jeanne Krug, 1915

military authorities ordered complete civilian evacuation. Forced to leave, she went to Paris – where the young Paul lived throughout the war with his grandmother – until, at the end of the year, she was allowed back into Reims. When the War ended she was prominent in founding the *Retour à Reims,* a body devoted to the problems of returning soldiers, prisoners-of-war or refugees – whether of rehousing, settling, employment, wounds, illnesses or missing relations. For her work in all these capacities she was awarded the Croix de Guerre and made a Chevalier of the Légion d'Honneur.

She had, too, at the closest quarters, the problems of the returning Joseph. He had contracted double pneumonia in the prisoner-of-war camp and had been sent to Switzerland for treatment in a pulmonary clinic. He was still extremely ill when he returned, and the business faced a whole series of problems. There were three compensations. In the first place, wartime restrictions of transport and trade meant that the stocks in the cellars were larger than in 1914; and there were three fine vintages, in quality if not in quantity, in 1919, 1920 and 1921. Significantly, domestic demand began to show an appreciable increase. Many of the French buyers, too, were drinking it *'à l'Anglaise'* – dry, before and during the meal, instead of after it – which made for a greater *per capita* consumption. Depressingly, however, the traffic of war and the ravages of untreated phylloxera had reduced the yield of many of the best vineyards to miserable proportions.

In 1918 the 'front line' villages of the Montagne de Reims – Chamery, Chigny, Ludes, Mailly, Rilly, Trepail, Verzenay, Verzy and Villery-Marmery – produced 273,000 gallons of wine compared with an average of 1,056,000 gallons in earlier years of peace. Even on the other side of the Montagne, Ay, Vertus, Hautvillers and Epernay had suffered heavily, too, and production had fallen by almost two-thirds; in all, the Marne vineyards showed a drop from 8,800,000 gallons to 2,526,000.

The half-hysterical, post-armistice celebration of peace created a demand for champagne which the more conservative British wine merchants thought uncritical. It was, though, a demand capable of sustaining a steep price increase. British importers who had paid £4 10s a dozen in 1914, now found themselves paying £7 0s. Krug was (excellars) 5.28 francs in 1913; 5.48 francs in 1914; 7.69 francs in 1918; 4.90 francs in 1919 but 9.08 francs in 1920. In Champagne a number of growers and groups sought to exploit the situation by planting vines in the clay-soil pockets where the damp conditions enabled them to produce far greater bulk of fruit than was possible on the 'champagne chalk' but totally unfit for making champagne. Laws had rapidly to be framed to check this practice by limiting the permissible yield and by confining approval to vineyards which had been in production before 1914. In the meantime there was a shortage of high-quality grapes, which disturbed growers and shippers alike. The series of falls in the value of the franc from 1919 on through the 1920s made costing all but impossible. In 1914 it stood at 25 francs to the pound; by the end of 1919 it was 41 francs; at the end of 1920, 60 francs; while by 1927 it was 124 francs – a fifth of its pre-war value. Although this tended to make it easier to sell to Britain, it meant that, by the time payment reached the growers and shippers for their grapes and/or bottles, it was not enough to cover the cost of the next year's production. The opulent Russian market disappeared – presumably for ever – with the 1917 Revolution.

In 1920, too, the United States of America – one of the largest markets for champagne – introduced Prohibition and Sweden was contemplating similar legislation. In the final outcome, that law had relatively little effect on champagne sales to the United States of America. Although anyone with a knowledge of human nature might have guessed, as one could foresee that, during the thirteen years until the aggressively puritanical Volsted

Act or 'Eighteenth Amendment' was repealed, bootleg-
gers – or rum-runners – imported as much champagne into
the United States of America as had gone in under legal
auspices before the War.

Even the British celebration was checked and, as if to
add to the French sense of grievance, it was done by one of
the most enthusiastic connoisseurs of champagne, Winston
Churchill. The duty on champagne had already gone up
from the pre-war 7s 6d to £1 11s a case, and as Chancellor
of the Exchequer in 1924, he imposed an *ad valorem* tax,
arguing that the wealthy should pay more on the best
champagne than the poor on cheap sparkling wine. The
tax lasted only a year but it was an added trial to the
shippers.

Joseph II made a valiant attempt to cope with these
troubles: but it is unlikely that he could have overcome
them without the assistance of his wife. Jeanne Krug was a
woman of keen intellect, controlled determination, and
considerable resilience. The firm's successes in the immediate post war period were a shared achievement. In
1919 Joseph directed the blending of 209,600 bottles for
other shippers; the next year 359,194 bottles were sold
under the Krug *marque*: the 1913, 1914 and 1915 vintages
were backed in the cellars by those of 1916 and 1917.
Neither in 1922 nor 1923 did Krug supply any wine to
other houses. Sales languished over the next couple of years
as Prohibition took effect and bootlegging was not yet
sufficiently well organized to compensate for the loss of
legitimate sales. When the runners completed their
operational plans, they ordered the champagne perfectly
legally to be sent to various territories round the United

States of America which did not come under that jurisdiction. If this meant that in some instances thousands of cases were ordered for a small island which had never bought champagne before, the houses could hardly be expected to worry. That they did not worry is indicated by the 'League of Opponents of Prohibition'. At the request of their customers many houses packed the bottles in unlabelled containers which were waterproofed so that, in the event of their being delivered and 'cellared' in some shallows outside the three-mile limit, or landed in the nets of fishing boats, the contents would not be damaged.

Joseph II's doctors now doubted if his health would allow him to continue to deal with the affairs of the firm. Since Paul was only twelve, it was obvious that a regent must be appointed. Accordingly, in 1924 – and with typical Krug family feeling – they appointed Jean Seydoux as joint manager. Jean was Joseph II's nephew and the

Jean Seydoux

senior of his many godchildren. His family lived almost next door, at 36 Boulevard Lundy where a wall plaque now commemorates Jean's youngest brother Roland, a member of the Resistance. He died in a German gas-chamber at Struthoff Camp in Alsace in 1944.

Like his co-manager, Jean Seydoux had a good palate, was an apt student of blending and, also like Joseph, he was an easy-going man. In the business he was valuable for his organising ability; he kept the establishment and its affairs in exemplary order; and he was a faithful friend – a genuine member of the family – during his thirty-eight years with the firm.

Most happily the doctors were proved wrong. Joseph II grew steadily fitter, resumed control of the business, and maintained it until 1959 when, at the age of ninety, he passed it on to Jean Seydoux and Paul II. At that point he became technical adviser to Krug et Cie, a post he occupied until his death in 1967, ninety-seven years old, having enjoyed a bonus of over forty years on the doctors' estimates.

When he resumed control he encountered unforeseen obstacles. Apart from 1922 and 1927, the vintages of the 1920s were good to outstanding in quality, though not large, since replanting after phylloxera was still in progress. Those of 1926 and 1928 were two of the finest ever made by Krug; and they are recalled now as among the best champagnes ever produced by any house. It hardly mattered that 1930 was indifferent, for stocks of high quality champagne were in the cellars. Then, in 1931, Britain went off the gold standard. To the champagne shipper that meant in effect a loss of 33 per cent unless prices were raised; and this at a time when Britain and the British Commonwealth were by far the biggest importers of his product. To increase prices would have been to destroy completely a market which was already wilting tragically. For the champagne trade in general it meant a damaging blow. In 1914 two-thirds of champagne production was exported; in the decade from 1930, the figure fell to an average of a third. For the *grandes marques* as a whole the proportion exported had been 50 per cent; for Krug always nearer 85 per cent. So the British currency crisis, coming on top of the French, demanded weighty consideration of the firm's policy. In 1929 the price was higher than it had ever been before at 21.30 francs a bottle; 193,368 bottles were sold against a general average of 225,000 since 1919. The merits of the Krug organisation were never more clearly apparent than now. It was essentially a family business; and, as they happily pointed out, a *bourgeois* family, always solvent, expanding only out of its own resources; never in debt, and always with stocks and capital in reserve. In 1931 Joseph II reduced the price to 17.62 francs a bottle and sold 144,351; in 1932 to 9.58 francs and sold 174,625 (in that year the firm made 86,581 bottles for others). The next year, out of pure economic necessity, the price had to go up to 15.09 francs. Nevertheless, largely in consequence of the repeal of the 'pussyfoot' Prohibition – Eighteenth Amendment in the United States of America – there was a sales recovery to 230,928 bottles. Another rise to 18.10 francs, two years steady at about 23 francs: in 1937 when 198,690 bottles went to other houses, sales for the first time amounted to over 10,000,000 francs. Then 1938 and 1939 were years of prosperity on the brink of war; 256,565 bottles at 37.17 francs; and 296,461 bottles at a new high price – soon to seem pitifully low – of 40.41 francs a bottle.

These were the hard figures which both shaped and reflected the progress of a genuinely personal business which was constantly and powerfully influenced by forces quite unrelated to its ideals or its product. It was always to resist the power of any great impersonal organisation to absorb it or to dictate its policy. In 1933, at twenty-one, his military service complete, Paul II for the first time joined his father and Jean Seydoux at a tasting, with ample time to learn the business and absorb its ethics under them before the full responsibility of the house devolved on him.

An extremely revealing glimpse of the way the business was run in the 1930s is afforded by the correspondence files. On 9 September 1936 a telegram from Reid, Pye and Campbell ran – 'Ship one triple magnum or larger Krug 1926 or earlier to arrive here Tuesday 15'. The order was placed for the firm of Fender, Tennyson, Yetts and Mills. The first two in the partnership were both Test cricketers. The Hon. Lionel – later Lord – Tennyson, who captained both Hampshire and England, was a huge, hearty extrovert, more brave than subtle, a fine trencherman and drinker. Percy George Fender, still well known in the London wine trade at eighty-two, was the nimble-witted captain of Surrey and an England all-rounder. He is credited with the remark, while tasting an over-chaptalized *bourgeois* claret – 'You know this is so sweet you could call it a *bourgeoise*'. The triple magnum was duly made up from other bottles – Krug never normally used any container bigger than a magnum – and dispatched in time to meet the order. The consequent account was for £2 3s. No 1926 Krug has appeared in a Christie's sale in recent years, but the last of the 1928 vintage to come up – in 1971 – made £285 a dozen, or nearly £24 a bottle: more than twice as much as any other modern champagne in their records. So, if that triple magnum of the 1926 is still undrunk ... The Fender, Tennyson firm were, in fact, good customers of Krug; often they ordered as much as a hundred cases at a time. Incidentally Reid, Pye and Campbell's account with Krug for that year was £46,404.

Joseph Krug II became one of the most respected and best-liked members of the champagne community. His years as a prisoner-of-war made a mark on him; sometimes he became restless, erratic, needed to get away. At first his family were alarmed by the fact that he would suddenly disappear, going off alone, sometimes for a week or more, skiing or mountaineering. He had an immense capacity for appreciation; his interest was kindled by a wide array of subjects – flowers, especially roses, antiquarian books but new books, as well, about any topic that caught his fancy, pictures, clogs, photography (he acquired a panoramic camera which delighted him) and, of course, champagne. He could never bring himself to drive a car, though he was often driven. He preferred a bicycle, and rode one until he was eighty.

After the war of 1914–18, Joseph Krug was invited to become a director of the Banque Chapuis which had always had heads of leading champagne houses – as well as other eminent Reims industrialists – on its board. He accepted, took his duties seriously, and was made a vice-president. Characteristically it never occurred to the man who was 'too nice to be in business' that the post – from which he could observe that the bank was being properly administered – could commit him to any financial liability. It was a normally sound, secure, concern. Its troubles stemmed from completely unforeseen – and unforeseeable – causes. After the First World War the French government issued cashable bonds to rebuild and reinstate industrial premises which had been damaged by enemy action. The number of bonds issued was huge; and they represented an operation the Banque Chapuis – like any other – was not organized to handle. Crucially, one of its executives recognized the criminal opportunity implicit in the situation. In short, the Banque Chapuis was ruined and the directors were responsible to its investors for their losses. Collectively they subscribed 80 per cent of the deficiency. Over a period of years and with difficulty, Joseph Krug, philosophically and unostentatiously, paid the full 100 per cent of his liability, which was a serious proportion of all he possessed. For Paul Krug II, a youth at the time, it was a salutary lesson: it taught him, he says, 'Never to promise – certainly never to be a bank director'.

In 1934 Walter Berry, the literarily inclined senior partner of Berry Bros and Rudd, made an enviable eight-week tour of the French vineyards, equipped with car, chauffeur and enough introductions to cover every stage of his itinerary. His record of that journey, *In Search of Wine*, contains a glimpse of Joseph Krug and his 'wonderful lady' at Reims, where he was welcomed, shown round the cellars, taken on visits he asked for to the Charbonneaux bottle-making plant and the Tassigny firm of cork-factors. Even more impressively, Joseph entertained the entire

Joseph Krug II, 1960

Berry party of four to both lunch and dinner with a selection of wines which reads like a parade of great vintages. Berry recalled that they were cheerfully welcomed by a large sheepdog and that, at coffee, a small terrier entertained them with some of its tricks.

Ian Maxwell Campbell, the son of Colonel Fred Campbell and his successor in Reid, Pye and Campbell, was not only the British agent for Krug, but an enthusiast for it. In *Reminiscences of a Vintner* he recalls two contacts with Joseph II which left deep impressions on him. During the inter-war years he organized the erection of a memorial to the 51st Highland Division at Beaumont-Hamel on the Somme, where its men had performed outstandingly during the First World War. The attendance of the Highland and military hierarchy was to be expected as their duty; Colonel Campbell was clearly touched by the fact that Joseph Krug and André Simon also appeared to pay their respects. He recalls, too, of 1947,

'Just before I celebrated my seventy-eighth birthday and he his seventy-ninth, I received a letter from my old friend Joseph Krug, begging me to delay no longer in coming over to Reims "before we both look too old" he added in his whimsical way. This appeal to the loyalty of friendship was irresistible, and over we went, my wife and I, and what a warmth of welcome and, may I say it, affection met us. . . .'

The Second World War was only initially a survival exercise for the Krug household. After 1940 they did remarkably well for a firm compelled to sell three-quarters of its production to Germany. Jean Seydoux became a leading member of the CIVC – the *Comité Interprofessionel du Vin de Champagne* – which, founded in wartime, guided the champagne trade through some of its most difficult years. Its official head is the Government Commissioner appointed by the Agriculture Ministry; his function is to hold a balance, when necessary, between the two constituent bodies of the Committee. They are the *Syndicat Générale des Vignerons,* founded in 1904 to protect the growers and now representative of all sectors in the vineyards; and the *Union des Syndicats du Commerce* which is the organ of the 144 champagne houses. No other organization the wine field has known ever received such a degree of cooperation from both growers and makers. As a member of its Consultative Commission, Jean Seydoux – too old for the army in the Second World War – devoted considerable skill to keeping good champagne out of the hands of the Germans. He was one of those who, from time to time, conducted negotiations with 'the Führer of Champagne'.

The champagne trade at first regarded the appointment of von Klaebisch to oversee their affairs under the Germans with some relief. He was a member of a Rhine wine family (his brother was made Führer of Cognac) and it was thought that he would be sympathetic. In the outcome, his superiors – or he succeeded in conveying that it was his superiors – made him a harsh taskmaster. The first allocation of all champagne was to the German armed forces; and sales to French civilians had to be authorized by von Klaebisch. On one occasion when three representatives of the CIVC were with him, he informed them that the Gestapo had ordered their arrest; and one of them, Comte Robert-Jean de Vogüé of Moët et Chandon was sentenced to death. A group of the major houses were heavily fined for protesting against the decision; but the Germans, with no troops to spare to quell an internal upheaval, never carried out the sentence. The CIVC did, too, succeed in winning some concessions from the 'Führer', notably permission to sell a quarter of each year's production in France and Belgium and to neutral Sweden, Finland and Switzerland.

In 1940, at the beginning of the German occupation, Joseph II noted with some anxiety the 20,000 to 25,000 bottles of the legendary Krug 1928 paid for by British customers of Reid, Pye and Campbell and marked in his cellars 'Paid for but not despatched'. As the property of British firms, it would have been legitimate German spoils of war. Assessing the situation, he counter-invoiced the wines and paid for them a second time with his own, personal, cheque, so that they became his property. As such he did not have to return them on the firm's inventory which the German occupying force demanded to be returned monthly. Perhaps von Klaebisch was not such an informed connoisseur as he might have been in the post he occupied. Oddly enough he never asked Joseph Krug whether he had any of his '28. If he had, he would have been told that it was the *gérant's* own personal property. In the event, when war ended Joseph, through Reid, Pye and Campbell offered all the '28 to the original purchasers at the original purchasing price. Incredible as it now seems, three-quarters of them – for what seemed to them good commerical reasons – refused that unique wine and asked instead for an allowance of later vintages. For that reason only there remain to this day, in the Krug family cellars, some historic bottles which, in commercial fact, were sold almost forty years ago.

Jean Seydoux's tact and organizing ability were of immense value to the firm during the war years. On the outbreak of war Paul II was commissioned into the Intelligence Corps of the French Army and attached to the British Forces HQ. He retreated with them, was evacuated through Dunkirk and was one of the many French servicemen who – like many others of various nationalities – with no clear picture of the situation in May 1940, were repatriated. In occupied France he returned to work in the business, strove to maintain communications between members of the family, including his wife (he and Jacqueline Fort were married in 1935) and young children, who had been evacuated to the South.

Meanwhile, on a more profoundly human level, Joseph II, the memory and emotions of his captivity during the First World War still sharp, and his wife were

active in maintaining escape routes – generally via Spain –
for members of the Allied forces – especially air crew – who
were at precarious liberty in France. They were both
arrested by the Gestapo but, after some time in prison at
Châlons-sur-Marne, nothing more than strong suspicion
could be levelled at them, and they were released.
Undeterred by their narrow escape, or the fact that they
were under suspicion, they continued their activities.
Madame Krug was arrested once more and this time she
was not released, but after imprisonment at Châlons was
committed to Fort Romainville near Paris where she was
held until she became seriously ill. Fortunately she was too
ill to be sent to Germany – as the Germans intended – on
the deportee train, stopped through the intercession of the
Swedish consul in Paris, Nordling, before it crossed the
frontier on its way to the extermination camp. Instead she
was one of the sick left, horrifyingly, under the surveil-
lance of Mongol guards. When the war ended she came
home a sick woman; but that did not prevent her from
working once more with *le Retour à Reims*, as she had done
after the previous war. The Médaille de la Résistance
completed a group of three awards quite exceptional for a
civilian – man or woman – in the two wars.

The pressures of war changed the trading pattern of the
House of Krug. Pre-eminently an exporting house, the
previous main markets of their history, in Britain and the
Commonwealth, were closed to them for five years. They
were flexible enough to maintain a steady flow of business,
despite the wartime handicaps of shortage of labour, with
consequent deterioration of the vineyards, lack of
experienced hands at the *vendange* and during vinification,

German depredations, the ageing of the vines, and bombing.

True to its history, champagne in the immediate post-war period surprised everyone who might have been expected best to understand it and its future. Instead of a sudden, semi-hysterical burst of celebration and a rapid recession, as was generally anticipated, both home and export sales grew steadily for more than twenty years. By Krug standards, peace found them in a poor position: they were a million bottles short of their criterion of six bottles in reserve for every one sold. They felt they were losing business and standing because they could not fulfil orders: yet they would not buy other champagne and put their label on it – as they could have done, easily and profitably – to satisfy the demand.

In 1945, the last half year of war in Europe, Krug sold 222,069 bottles; 193,909 bottles – 67 per cent – of them in France. In 1946, of 227,030 bottles sold, 148,234 – 65 per cent – were exported. A large proportion of the exported wine went to England, and the firm's French agents resented the switch.

The elders of Reid, Pye and Campbell recall 'the Krug train' of the immediate post-war years. In early spring the rail trucks were loaded in the goods yard a few hundred metres behind Rue Coquebert with 6,000 to 8,000 cases of champagne to make a train which was routed direct to Dieppe, where the cargo was transferred to the boat for Newhaven. Sometimes a spring frost would send the agents' representatives hurrying down to Sussex to improvise heating in the warehouses and customs sheds lest the wine should come to harm. That was their only possible concern. They did not need to handle the wine; it was all sold – or, to be accurate, allocated, for hardly a customer could have as much as he wanted – before it arrived. Reid, Pye and Campbell had only to supervise the distribution. Their main anxiety was to prevent trading in the 'script' – when some wholesalers used to sell their allocation to others at a premium without even taking delivery of it: while others, again, held it as an investment which would appreciate in value.

Some stocks of the 1937 and 1938 remained; 1940 was ready; 1941, 1942, 1943, 1945 and, soon, 1947 were fine – if not large – vintages building up in the cellars. Importantly, when the price of grapes rose in a small, high-quality vintage, Krug did not hesitate to bid for the best grapes.

Prices – of grapes, labour, bottles, corks, printing, transport – continued to rise. So did the price of champagne; 40 francs in 1939; 63 francs in 1943 when, for the first time, Krug sales rose above 20,000,000 francs; 129 francs in 1945; 254 francs in 1946, with receipts over 55,718,000 francs. It was a helter-skelter progress which no one could halt.

Since 1937 Krug have made no champagne for other houses. In the later 1940s and the 1950s the firm ticked comfortably along. Neither Joseph II nor Jean Seydoux was competitive; neither did they perceive the need to compete.

Madame Krug never recovered her health after her imprisonment; and she died in 1954. In 1959 Joseph II gave up control of the firm. He did not withdraw completely, and often into the 1960s three generations of the family – Joseph II, Paul II, Henri and Rémi – might be seen together in the offices or tasting-room as well as on domestic occasions. Jean Seydoux died in 1962 and Paul II became sole *gérant* of the House of Krug.

On 6 July 1967 a photograph was taken in the old garden of '*le Quarante*' of Joseph II with André Simon (then ninety) who had asked particularly to see him and who called – surely to their mutual sense of occasion – at eleven in the morning, champagne time in the wine world. André Simon's last volume of autobiography, *In the Twilight*, contains: 'We were hospitably entertained by members of the present day generation of the champagne trade, but there were no more than two of real age with whom to talk about olden days: Princesse Henri de Polignac and Joseph Krug. My old friend Joseph Krug, now ninety-eight years old, was wonderful when we called at eleven o'clock. We had a bottle of Krug 1955 together. He stood up erect, remembered names and dates. I was astounded then, and greatly shocked when, some two weeks later, I learnt that he had died in his sleep.'

IO

Paul II: the perfectionist

There was never any doubt that Paul II would become the head of the family champagne house. Joseph I and Paul I could not be born into the Krug tradition for the simple reason that they created it. Joseph II had a warm family feeling, but he accepted the succession to the *marque* as an obligation. Paul II, born into it, recognized its growing strength, embraced it and devoted himself to it.

Physically he resembles his grandfather, conveying an impression of power, and with an aura of determination. To a greater extent than any of his relations, he has a feeling for history in the wider as well as the family scene – and his researches into the Krug archives have increased his devotion to the concept of continuity. It is both his strength and his weakness that he is profoundly emotionally involved in his business.

When he took control he could, and did, look back. The meticulous figures of those generations of German and Swiss clerks gave him much to ponder. Above all, he had to accept that the history of the champagne trade is one of change and constantly fresh problems.

Each of the Krug *gérants* in his turn had acute difficulties – always different from those of his predecessor. Joseph had to establish himself, to organize foreign markets and to weather a Revolution, the American and European economic crises of 1857 and 1858 and the heavy loss of exports due to the American Civil War. Even in the era of prosperity, Paul I had to deal with the repercussions of the Franco-Prussian War and with phylloxera. Joseph II was absent because of one World War, and in control through the other, and suffered the impact of the growers' discontent.

Paul II was – and is increasingly after more than a dozen years – faced with the problem of competition of new kinds in conditions favourable to his competitors. In essence his problem is that posed to all the old champagne houses: which is, simply enough, whether there is a permanently viable place for a true champagne – the skilful blend of different, good quality black and white grapes from Champagne vineyards, subjected to all the established processes and faithfully matured – in face of the competition of one-vineyard or one-village champagnes and, even more, of the sparkling wines which, because of advances in modern technological chemistry, all the winefields of the world can produce with increasing efficiency, and at a price no more than a fraction of that of champagne.

On the surface the new *gérant* had every reason to be content. On 1 January 1962, the year of his accession to full authority, yet another warrant from a British monarch appointed the House 'the place and quality of Purveyors of

Champagne to Her Majesty'. Sales figures moved fairly steadily ahead as far as 481,926 bottles – the highest annual return since 1910 – in 1973.

Crucially, though, even this did not keep proportional pace with the rise in consumption either of champagne or of sparkling wines in general. Increasingly champagne, especially the finest, was becoming isolated in several sectors. On average, Champagne produces and sells 125 million bottles a year; Krug's figure is less than half a million. Krug is one of the *grandes marques*; the *grandes marques* are twelve of the 144 registered champagne houses. In a trend André Simon identified a decade ago as 'one of the most spectacular changes to take place in the champagne trade since the First World War' the *vignerons – récoltants-manipulants* – have been responsible for a steadily growing proportion of champagne sales. André Simon

The yard at 5 Rue Coquebert

showed how their share had increased from some 8 per cent to over 20 per cent by 1960. Since Paul Krug II has been in control of Krug, the figure has moved up until, by 1973, it was 28 per cent (34,700,000 bottles to 90,000,000 bottles).

Almost all the *récoltants-manipulants'* champagne is single-grape, single-vineyard, perhaps single-village; generally it is young and sweet, calculated to appeal to the taste of the central French and Belgian tourists who visit the vineyards.

This is internal *Champenois* competition. Export sales are a separate question. In 1973 the *récoltants-manipulants* had almost 40 per cent of champagne sales in France but, of the export market, only 2 per cent. Meanwhile in the British market, traditionally the biggest for champagne, its share of the sales of sparkling wine fell from 52 per cent in 1971 to 40 per cent in 1973.

Since the Second World War the consumption of wine in Britain has increased rapidly, though not along traditional lines. The greater part of the new purchasing power lies in the lower price brackets. Thus, while in the years 1972 and 1973, champagne sales increased by 15 per cent and 2 per cent; the other – non-champagne – sparkling wines made immense advances. French (non-champagne) sparkling wine moved up 41 per cent and 53 per cent; German by 14 per cent and 39 per cent; Spanish, despite fiscal discrimination, 40 per cent and 75 per cent. In view of the historic 'Spanish Champagne' case, those figures are ironic.

The Wine and Spirit Association's objective survey observes, coolly, 'A price explosion which amounted to

72 per cent between 1972 and the first half of 1974 still left champagne in short supply in the United Kingdom market. The long term outlook is for a continued rise in price and continued shortage.' Referring to 'functions and discriminating private drinkers supplied through traditional channels' it concludes that 'This section is turning to wines prepared by the *méthode Champenoise* which are meeting the needs of frustrated champagne drinkers.'

The 'frustrated champagne drinkers' must concern every producer of champagne. Of all champagne, 33 per cent is exported; of the *grandes marques*, 50 per cent; of Krug – like Bollinger and Veuve Clicquot – 75 per cent, until last year when the proportion fell to 60 per cent. Paul Krug, looking up from his books in October 1974, remarked 'sales are growing in Canada and Venezuela – everywhere else they are shrinking – even in the United States of America and France.' The competition now is not primarily that between the houses and the *négociants-manipulants,* but between champagne and the sparkling wines of the rest of the world. Even in France sales of champagne fell 9 per cent between 1972 and 1974: the houses lost almost 7,000,000 bottles; the *négociants* and cooperatives about 3,000,000 bottles. The export figure fell about 25 per cent; the houses' from 38,786,733 to 29,254,795 bottles; the *récoltants* and cooperatives from 915,700 to 660,517 bottles. These are ominous figures for the former competitors, who may yet find themselves partners in a dilemma.

Every champagne shipper has had to adjust his procedure to meet changing circumstances. The case of Krug is not quite identical with the majority of the *grande marques,* most of whom have long had vineyards of their own. The Krug concept was always one of separate functions within the *vignoble* – growers grew grapes and makers made wine. It must be significant that, for whatever reason Paul I bought the Mailly vineyards – and such was his wealth that it may have been simply to help a landowner friend who needed money – he sold them, despite the high standing of their grapes, apparently without regret. There is no doubt that all the family down to Paul II held the same point of view; and that he himself did so until about 1960. He had thought the CIVC largely a wartime measure and that, with the end of war, the more restrictive regulations would be relaxed. The reverse proved the case. His hope was that he would again be able to buy grapes of his choice, when he would not quibble about the price. It was long a Krug maxim that 'a good lunch between shippers and growers is essential for their relations' but the essential quality of Krug champagne lies in their freedom to choose the constituent grapes. Now, while it is necessary to belong to the CIVC to buy grapes, membership does not automatically give the maker the freedom to buy the particular grapes he wants. The shippers need coupons to buy them; and the coupons are allocated by the CIVC with due consideration for the interests of the growers: so that it is often obligatory for shippers to buy grapes they do not want in order to be allowed to buy some of those they do want.

The situation is worked out in detail by the CIVC, but for our purpose here it is sufficient that roughly the grapes of half the planted surface of Champagne are 'engaged', which means that the growers are under contract to deliver them at the agreed price to the shippers to whom they have been allocated. About a third of the fruit grown is used for their own wine by growers, cooperatives or unions; a sixth goes into the free market – where shippers can compete for their own choice – but with a guaranteed minimum.

Against this background Joseph II, Paul II and Jean Seydoux decided in 1960 that the firm would buy vines. This involved two major changes of policy. The first was that of owning vines at all; the second, even more fundamental, was the opening of the business to interests outside the family for – apart from the original involvement of de Vivès – the first time. That decision was imposed by the simple fact that the funds of the Krug's domestic business were inadequate for the operation it needed to undertake. As a result, the cognac house of Remy Martin and the liqueur manufacturers, Cointreau – both of whom share several views on commercial principle with Krug – took shares in the firm.

Their joint holding amounts to 35 per cent of the equity; Paul Krug II's immediate family owns another 35 per cent; his three surviving aunts and numerous cousins the remaining 30 per cent. Thus, if a divisive issue should arise, the family group is effectively in control of the House. So far nothing of that nature has occurred. There have been some changes in organisation; representatives of the seventy-strong staff in Reims – workers and clerks – have seats on the board; Krug became a limited company in 1928; a *Société Anonyme* in 1970; Paul Krug was elected a *gérant* for life in 1941, but as the Chairman of Krug SA he, like the managers, must be re-elected every six years.

In 1973 Paul Krug invited all the members of the family

who had inherited an interest in the firm – with their husbands, wives or fiancées – to a party of inspection of the firm's resources. Two motor coaches collected them in Paris and transported them to Rue Coquebert and then to the newly purchased Villedommange properties, where the catering facilities provided a meal – served with Krug. The founder of the feast surveyed the vast number of his shareholders, gathered together for the only time in history, and felt paternally content.

From Jean Seydoux's death in 1962, Paul II ran the company alone until 1965. He could have his father's advice – when he asked for it – otherwise all was left to him. Meanwhile his sons were being trained for the business. The two, different in character, were also prepared differently for their parts. They were sent to England to learn the language of the House's main market; there was travel, training in management, economics and commercial practice. Henri came into the business as a junior in 1962 when he was twenty-five; Rémi in 1965, at twenty-three. Each, after five years, was made a joint manager equally with Paul II, the elected chairman. Their duties are clearly defined. Paul II directs overall policy. Henri, serious, painstaking, concerned with technique and organization, is usually to be found in the office or the vineyards. Rémi, volatile and extrovert, is responsible for marketing and public relations. At the spring blending all three taste; but Paul II takes the ultimate decision. He plans to retire within the next few years but already the two younger men, like each of the previous generations in the business, have been directed and established – Paul insists that 'it is not a succession, it is a progression'. Their

Four generations – Joseph II, Paul II, Henri, Olivier

relationship is a strikingly smooth one; there is sympathetic division of labour and responsibility; and general agreement – 'When one Krug answers, he answers for all.' The three have already shared a considerable amount of modernization in which they have striven to balance high quality production with growth in sales and profitability.

Henri's task has lain largely in the field of negotiation for the grapes the firm wants at a price it can pay. Rémi's has been that of organizing sales-points and methods to fit the changing pattern of champagne drinking. In England, for instance, the chief purchasers of Krug used to be the London clubs where considerable quantities of champagne had been drunk since Edwardian times. It was sold in the more expensive hotels and restaurants, while an appreciable section of the privileged bought it in fairly generous quantities from their one-shop family wine-merchants for their domestic use. Clubs and club life have both changed markedly; champagne-drinking is no longer habitual among any substantial proportion of members. High prices have affected restaurant sales, while apparently encouraging them in night clubs which formerly used only to keep the cheaper *marques*. Most of the noble and wealthy families of Edwardian days have bowed in some way or other to the pressure of taxation. The single-shop wine merchants now supply only a small proportion of British wine-drinkers. As with all wines, too, there has been a significant switch to home consumption. This is partly explained by the high mark-ups in restaurants, and partly by the television-induced tendency to drink and dine at home rather than elsewhere. Krug can now be bought at an increasing number of 'popular' shops; and it is available to all the 'chains'. Although the three accepted this line of development, they decided not to 'popularize' the wine. There would be no 'gimmicks' of packaging or pre-sentation, no lowering of sights. Indeed, in 1973, Rémi composed a statement on the firm's code of standards – the use exclusively of Marne grapes; fermentation in cask; traditional *remuage*; homogeneous corks; racking, disgorging, dosage, checking and final corking carried out individually and by hand; and a six-year storage of all bottles before they are sold – to explain the high cost of Krug.

Krug is – and has been through its finest days – the wine of privilege. Among its potential purchasers, however, privilege has not been constant. It is no longer the 'accepted' champagne in all the places where it can be bought; the night clubs now know it; some of the 'chains' are beginning to recognize it; and it is there that the holding operation must be carried out. Paul II recognizes it as a task for the younger generation, which has grown up in the atmosphere that produced the situation.

Sales of all champagne are falling dramatically. Even in Champagne itself, no one knows why: and they have decided to conduct a market research to discover the cause. Formerly, Paul I could explain a poor year with a laconic word or two – 'war' or 'commercial crisis' – in the final column of his statistical account of the firm's progress. This time the reason is more complex.

While the general problem of competition is one for all champagne, it makes different impacts on different sections of the trade. The *récoltants-manipulants,* for instance, are little concerned – for the moment – with the export market; while the shippers are content to leave the localized tourist sales to the *vignerons.* The *récoltants-manipulants* have made a significant impact on French shop trade; but essentially their output hovers between the full, blended and matured champagne of the shippers and the sparkling wines of other areas. In effect they are trading – justifiably and legally enough – on the name-value of champagne. Since they are vinifying their own grapes, which are not, for their purpose, subject to the decreed basic charge which applies to shippers, they can sell their wine more cheaply than the shippers. On the other hand, it would be uneconomic for them to set the price so low that it would be more profitable to them to sell the grapes to the shippers: therefore they can never undersell the mass-produced sparkling wines at their skilfully cut prices.

In short, whatever approach anyone in Champagne chooses to make to the present dilemma, champagne which conforms to the wine laws can never be cheap enough to compete with the commercial 'sparklers' manufactured only a few kilometres outside the region.

The fixing of grape prices, based, essentially, on the premise of growers and shippers having separate and different interests, was the conclusive factor in ruling champagne out of all price-competition. It may, also, yet prove a decisive factor in establishing an appreciable price-differential between the product of the *récoltants-manipulants* – who stand halfway between one group and the other but belong, fundamentally, in the growers' camp – and the shipper.

Since the Second World War the prices of the scheduled 100 per cent champagne grapes have been:

1946   70 francs (old francs, for comparison, 0.70 NF)
1956   132 francs (1.32 NF)
1966   3.10 NF (new francs)
1970 4.27 NF
1971 4.66 NF
1972 5.33 NF
1973 6.37 NF
1974 7.37 NF

Thus the cost has multiplied tenfold since 1946, almost doubled in the past six years.

So, if there was one course the shippers could not take, it was to make effectively cheap champagne. Some champagne – especially that of the lesser vineyards or the *premier* and *deuxième tailles* – has always been significantly poorer and cheaper than, not only the best, but also the medium quality 'shippers' product. Indeed, there exists a recognized second quality, usually sold as BOB – 'Buyers Own Brand' – which bears the name of the retailer, wine merchant, hotel or restaurant because the original maker is reluctant to put his own name on it. It is what the makers call 'wedding champagne', and say is 'all right for christening enemy ships'.

It is possible to identify the source of champagne from the label. In small type, next to the licence number, it must bear the letters 'NM' (*Négociant Manipulant*) if the name on the label is that of the maker; or 'MA' (*Marque d'acheteur*) if it is labelled for the buyer. Even BOB, though, is significantly dearer than simple sparkling wine from other regions.

In order to enter present-day competition, some houses have created dual or even triple standards in their own wines; generally non-vintage, vintage and *de luxe* versions, the last often specially packaged. Some have made a Blanc de Blancs solely from white grapes: it is an attractive light and delicate wine though it lacks the body of traditional champagne. Others have marketed the still wine which many houses have made on a small – often family – scale for years; it is deep, powerful and palatable; and, not strictly champagne, must be labelled *Coteaux Champenois*.

It would be imprecise to suggest that Paul Krug II rejected those courses – that would imply a negative approach. He was not prepared to lower his quality standards to enter the bracket of a cheap – or even a 'not-too-dear' – champagne. He decided to make what he considered the best champagne; and, if it happened also to be the dearest, he would not allow that fact to disturb him.

That may prove to have been a commercially sound course. If so, it will be partly coincidental, for it was taken less for commercial than for family and traditional reasons. If Paul Krug II were the disinterested managing director of a wine-making firm he would hardly have taken such a course. His attitude may be described as aggressive, defiant, purist or – as probably fits it best – élitist: its basic motive is family pride.

Few other houses have maintained the direct father–son line of descent throughout their history as Krug has done. In fewer – if any – has the head of the family always – without the aid of *chef de cave* or chemist – been completely responsible for the blending of every wine in the firm's history. Pride in ancestry is the foundation of the Krug attitude.

It is not easy – and certainly never cheap – to buy good, delimited, vineyards in Champagne. The first modern Krug purchase, in 1960, was the Roussin vineyard at Villedommange; about 5½ hectares with press house and a complex of buildings which have been turned into accommodation for *vendangeurs,* and offices. In 1971 and 1972 the firm added the – to use the house agents' word – 'desirable properties' at Ay of Edouard Besserat (4½ hectares) and Vignoble Gosset (8½ hectares); and, finally, the Tarin property at le Mesnil-sur-Oger (5½ hectares). This gave them some twenty-six hectares (sixty-four acres) of the finest grape-growing land in Champagne, at a cost of about £1m – and the admission of non-family interests to the company. The Clos du Mesnil – as its name implies, a walled vineyard – is the most striking of these acquisitions, since it is entitled to the exclusive *appellation contrôlée* of Clos du Mesnil.

These purchases by no means solve all the firm's problems of grape-supply. They ensure, however, that in a normal year, 30 per cent of the grapes they use – all among those they would ideally choose for their blend – come from their own vineyards. Still Paul insists 'We can always produce a better champagne than anyone else if we can sort the good from the bad – the problem is not to *see* the grapes you want, but to *buy* them.'

The future of the region cannot be clearly foreseen. Champagne, as this generation knows it, is a relatively young wine. In the century and a half since it became clear and sparkling in safe bottles, its grower-shipper relationship – unique among the winefields of the world – has been in unpredictable flux. In 1970 four of the *grandes marques* – Veuve Clicquot-Ponsardin, Roederer, Bollinger and Krug – formed a 'Group of Common Economic Interest'. Its purpose is to unite houses which have similar links with the growers, in case – which is an alarming thought – the CIVC should collapse or the government should cease to maintain it. Gradually, the factor of élitism became almost as much a method as an objective. Other houses might rationalise their processes, employing modern aids to reduce costs below those of the traditional methods. Paul II would do so only if he were convinced that the change would not impair quality in the slightest degree. Every time he rejected a possible simplification of method, he increased both his costs – in comparison with almost all his competitors – and the price of Krug champagne. He would have no *de luxe cuvée* or *sous marque*: there is only one Krug – the best he can possibly make – in any year.

From a fine harvest he will generally make a vintage wine. He is prepared to argue, though, that his *Private Cuvée*, using *cépages* from several different years, may be better than a vintage. He likes to compose a *cuvée* from a wider range of qualities than is likely to be found in any but a phenomenal single vintage. Lately he made up a blend for which a label was printed saying that it consisted of a choice of growths from the years 1970, 1969, 1968, 1967, 1966, 1965 and 1964. It was decided not to include that information because a vintage-conscious market might think a blend of such proportions in some way of lesser quality than that of a single year. That, of course, is not true, but Paul Krug doubts if the buying public is yet able to recognize the fact.

Paul II accepts his responsibility to buy the grapes the CIVC allocates to him. He merely reserves the right not to use those he considers unsuitable for his wine. In most years Krug pass on a considerable amount of wine to other houses because they do not choose to include it in their blends.

They will use only grapes from the Marne vineyards. Under the CIVC pricing, the various vineyards are assessed at between 100 per cent and 77 per cent. As a recent example, in 1969 the average was 86 per cent; the Krug purchases averaged 93 per cent – 'as always, we purposely included certain small vineyards of lesser classification; they have interesting characteristics which, in small quantities, help to create the individuality of our wine.' He demands rigorous selection; from an indifferent year he is content to make only a small *cuvée* from such good grapes as he can find. His insistence on *'épluchage'* – the picking out of the rotten grapes – adds to labour charges and reduces bulk. It is apparent at *vendange* time that Paul – or Henri – will demand *épluchage* at one vineyard and not at another because, although they must buy them, they do not intend to use the grapes of the second grower.

A first pressing – of the standard 4,000 kilogrammes of grapes – produces the *cuvée* and a proportion of the first *taille* from white grapes only. The remainder is sold to other makers. The eventual wine is not automatically sold as Krug: in 1967 30 per cent; in 1968, 20 per cent, was sold off.

Most champagne makers now ferment in high capacity, stainless steel vats instead of the traditional casks of oak – originally Hungarian, now from Argonne, Lorraine or Alsace. Only two houses – Krug and Bollinger – still use oak casks for their entire production. They believe that only slow, regular fermentation in wood ensures the finesse which is an important characteristic of the wines of both houses. Secondly, on a strictly practical level, the lower capacity of the cask permits, without undue financial penalty, the elimination of a single unsatisfactory unit in a *cuvée*. To reject the entire contents of a 7,000 gallon vat is a costly gesture, made only out of dire necessity. Finally, the smaller unit of the cask allows an imaginative palate in creating a wine which, at its best, blends the most appropriate available taste-colours into a rounded creation.

The firm has always cherished its old-established relationships, but the huge modern commercial complexes have swallowed up many local firms, like Debear, the Reims printers, who for years printed all the Krug labels, and the local bottle-makers. Some cork factors maintain the old links; cooperage, though, is a shrinking craft and Krug – although recognized as one of the best-paying employers among the houses – still consider themselves fortunate to have three experienced men to repair their casks.

Krug wine is never filtered; that might eliminate important factors: it is all hand-racked. Many modern cellars employ metal crown caps for wine between secondary fermentation and disgorging. Krug use full corks because they believe metal caps are not completely trustworthy and, though they are convenient for mechanized disgorging, dosage, and final corking, in the Krug establishment all those processes are carried out by hand so that each bottle can be checked at every stage.

The process of *remuage* – turning and shaking bottles to clear the sediment – can be reduced from five months to six weeks by adding Bentonite to each bottle. Krug add nothing; *remuage* takes place in the traditional manner. Indeed, in their cellars – since *remuage* is personal – each *remueur* has his own stacks which no one else is allowed to handle. He refers to them as 'my wines' and, if he goes on holiday, they remain untouched until his return.

The process of ageing by malolactic fermentation is now widely practised; if this occurs in any Krug wine, the cask is instantly discarded. The world shortage of mature cork has persuaded most champagne houses to use 'agglo' – cork agglomerate – for their bottles. Only two – Bollinger and Krug – insist on solid homogeneous cork – at three times the cost of 'agglo'. Krug use corks of four different gradings, according to the climate of the country where the wine

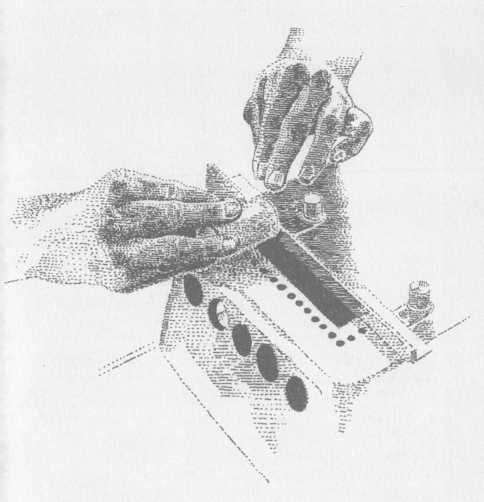

will be sold. Champagne stocks in general cover three years' sales: Krug always maintain a six-year cover. Their aim is to produce an ultimate small quantity of as fine a champagne as it is possible to make. That is their decision. The problems of selling it will not change their faith.

In 1975 and 1976 the falling value of the pound and the largest tax increase ever imposed on wine added to the difficulties of champagne sales to Britain, yet there was indication of improvement and total British sales increased by 4 per cent. The overall figures for 1975 showed a rise of one per cent which may sound small but, in terms of shipments, it means some 664,000 bottles. In France there was an impressive increase in all sales of 16 per cent, giving an aggregate figure of over fifty million bottles.

Talking then, Paul Krug still did not shift his ground. 'In the high quality field we are almost the only house left. If we change, or relax our standards, we merely join the group of long-established firms who are now competing for the middle-price market. We should be lost there. Marketing can do nothing for us; our strength and our hope for the future lie in our quality. We must maintain our standards in the hope that, even in a world beset by economic problems, there are still certain people who can distinguish between Krug and all other champagnes and esteem that difference sufficiently to pay for it. We know faithful people buy 400,000 bottles a year.'

The new arrangement with the growers – a guarantee to buy grapes equivalent to 80 per cent of shipments – worked well in 1975. By 1977 the entire question will come up again: so there is no assurance of security.

Meanwhile, continuing with the *Private Cuvée* – and, from time to time, a vintage – the House has introduced a *Crémant*. This is an altogether different wine; although it is made in Champagne it is not champagne. It is a lighter, more delicate, less sparkling wine, made from a preponderance of white grapes (three to one) whereas the

le Mesnil

normal Krug champagne is made from two of black to one of white. Selling in restaurants at about half the price of the *Private Cuvée*, it will take a great name into a lower price range without lowering the standard of the true product; so the campaign – or is it a mission? – continues.

Still problems remain; indeed they grow more complex and weighty. Paul Krug observes 'In every generation things have been getting worse; but we are still here.'

He is obviously accustomed to being asked what he would order in a restaurant which had no Krug. When he says 'A cup of tea', that is a 'front' reply. Discover him dining with his friend Victor Lanson and you will see him happily drinking his host's Black Label. That, however, must not be allowed to obscure his belief that Krug is – supremely – the finest champagne in the world.

11

The taste of Krug

To drink a great wine at its best, with a sympathetic accompaniment of food and company, in comfort and no haste, is one of the most profound of all physical pleasures. Indeed, sometimes it seems to transcend the realm of the physical.

Ernest Hemingway, the sentimentalist who wrote tough, examined and recorded human feeling with greater precision than most, and he did so characteristically in – 'Wine is one of the most civilized things in the world, and one of the material things of the world that has been brought to the greatest perfection, and which offers a greater range of enjoyment and appreciation than, possibly, any other purely sensory thing that may be purchased.'

There could be no better spokesman for champagne than André Simon, that enthusiastic, generous Frenchman who settled in England and, as well as acting as British representative for a champagne house, taught the British more about the civilisation of wine and food than any other dozen human beings in the history of the nation. He lived to the age of ninety-three and, since he was gloriously active with a glass until virtually the end, he must have drunk – and infallibly enjoyed – more champagne than all but a few people in the history of the wine. Perhaps he was less than a disinterested witness, but these words are truly in character – 'If champagne were but a luxury, an exhilarating, fascinating wine for festive occasions, it would be of little importance whether its consumption were limited by its high cost; but champagne is also the most wholesome of stimulants, the finest aid to digestion and the safest as well as the pleasantest medicine for depression and exhaustion. It is most unfair that it should be placed far beyond the means of all but surtax people. At the same time, it is as well to bear in mind that champagne can never be cheap, because it cannot be made without good people, much care, trouble and time. Cheap champagne is a contradiction in terms and an abomination.' Paul Krug II would undoubtedly agree with the last three sentences.

The best beer or whisky is a good drink; a great wine is a major experience. Rémi Krug expresses his belief in the wine which is his heritage, his career and in effect his mission, in four words 'the taste of Krug'. The forty-nine distinct and different blended wines – of Ay, Ambonnay, Oger, le Mesnil, Leuvrigny, Verzenay, Bouzy, Pouillon, Mailly, Villedommange, Sillery – merge into a single, distinct, unity of flavour unlike any of its components or any other champagne. Moreover, year in, year out, although the grapes sometimes come from different vineyards, although the weather and the quality of the harvest vary from year to year, that flavour remains constant, richer in some years, more austere in others; sometimes fuller, sometimes more powerful but always itself; unmistakeable. Drink it, as most of us do only once in months or years, and the flavour – though of a different year – *Private Cuvée* or vintage – is instantly and unmistakeably recognizable. It is simply the taste of Krug. It has been made in that character by four generations of the family; a fifth is at hand; and a sixth waits beyond.

The *Champenois* drink without ceremony, but with care, to make the best of their wine. In the Krug houses – of Paul II, Henri and Rémi – on three sides of the old rose garden of '*le Quarante*' they serve their champagne cellar-cool but never iced. In a restaurant Paul II will send back a bottle of Krug which has been over-chilled in an ice bucket. The imperfections of a bad champagne can be concealed by serving it almost frozen – but so can the merits of a fine champagne.

It is drunk from a tall, slim but ample, flute or tulip glass – never from one of the saucers-on-a-stem foisted on the British by keepers of Victorian knick-knack shops.

It is spectacular, but wasteful, to fire the cork into the air. Some can take it between the fingers and extract it smoothly with a twist of the wrist. Those who cannot may economically use one of the claw-shaped pincers made for the purpose, when, with a firm but unhurried turn, the cork may be released with, as it should be, no more than 'the full-breathed sigh of a satisfied woman'.

In the Krug household, it is drunk before – and with the first course of – lunch or dinner. After that the family generally drink claret. In that regard Paul II was fortunate

Jacqueline Krug

– or clever – to marry his eldest daughter, Christine, to Jean-Henri Schÿler, of the family and firm of Schröder et Schÿler, well known as Bordeaux *négociants* for more than two hundred years.

To write a book about a wine without discussing what it is like to drink is like the biography of a beautiful woman which makes no reference to her appearance. Yet the language of wine-tasting is imprecise, and it can all too easily become pretentious by taking its images from unrelated worlds. It is said that Brahms once visited some profoundly Rhineland endowed cellar where his host opened a bottle and poured him a glass with 'Mr Brahms, this bottle is to wine what Brahms is to music.' Thereupon the composer said 'In that case, I will thank you for a draught of Johann Sebastian Bach.'

Paul II, who makes it, says – 'Every one of the growths of the champagne vineyards is different in bouquet and taste from any other. Those differences are, in many cases, less attractive than they were because of over-production.

Selection becomes increasingly important because it is increasingly difficult. The characteristics of the poorer areas are heightened by excessive acidity; while unripe fruit simply has less taste than ripe. Our selection takes those factors into consideration; they are checked before blending begins. Krug is a full champagne with a full bouquet which is always clean and clear, however old the wine. This is because it is fermented in wood, and we take infinite care to keep out all impurities and we use virtually no chemical aids. So, when a bottle of Krug is twenty or thirty years old, its age may be apparent but it is still clean in bouquet and flavour.'

He feels that Krug in a bottle is at its best between seven and eight years old; magnums perfect at ten to fifteen. At times the firm has used imperial pints and imperial quarts as well as bottles, halves and magnums. Paul does not favour anything larger than a magnum – 'We have sometimes made up double, or even triple, magnums by decanting halves, to please friends who want to show off a bit – but that is not good for the wine.' He believes that half-bottles are simply 'no good'; and that the fashion – strong in the United States of America – for halves, can militate against a wine's reputation. He does not like to sell a wine – certainly not a vintage – less than six years old – 'We sell at the point when it is good to start drinking it.'

Michael Broadbent, of Christie's, who has an immensely wide range of tasting experience, a retentive palate-memory, high standards of comparison, keeps encyclopaedic notes, says 'Krug at its best and most mature is one of the greatest champagnes, if not *the* greatest. The finest champagne I have ever had in my life was Krug '28 (in 1957); Paul Krug produced it before lunch. As to its style – in appearance it is usually a pleasant, refreshing-looking straw-yellow with a hint of gold which deepens with age. The bubbles are small, consistent, even-floating. The *mousse* is lively but not frothy. The bouquet is usually rich and fragrant, characterful, "meaty" yet refreshing; sometimes with the noticeable "smoky" *pinot* character of a fine white burgundy. On the palate it is always dry, varying slightly between an austere dryness when young to a softer, medium-dryness when mature. It is always fairly full-bodied, without being heavy (except in the case of the 1959); rich yet low-keyed. What really distinguishes Krug is its refinement with concentration, and, above all, its pervasive, *long* flavour and almost attenuated long, dry finish. Krug is rich, refined, understated. Like a Lafite '45, if it is tasted superficially it may seem merely a nice wine; but, tasted carefully, it reveals richness, subtlety and depth. The weight of Krug varies with the vintages; 1959 was a heavyweight; 1952 light for Krug; 1953 lighter; 1955 "classic" in my opinion; 1961 firm and for maturing; 1962 a little austere. Krug of all champagne needs maturity. On two specific occasions I have noted Krug at peak fourteen years after the vintage. So, by my reckoning, 1961, 1962 and 1964 are all in the finest maturity bracket now, but if stored in properly cool cellars it will keep almost indefinitely – best of all in magnums.'

There is considerable British support for Michael Broadbent's superlatives about the Krug 1928. One comes in a diverting passage from Alec Waugh's *In Praise of Wine* – 'Middle age has its own rewards. A taste for champagne is one of them. In my twenties I despised it as a vulgar,

Paul Krug II

ostentatious drink. In my thirties I patronized it. But most men after forty, if they have not switched to spirits, find that champagne does something for them that no other wine can do. I was lucky in that my taste for it began to mature at the very moment in the late '30s when Krug 1928 was moving to its majestic peak. I do not expect to see a wine like that again, in its depth of colour, body and full-blooded fragrance.'

Maurice Healy, Irishman, barrister, wit and immense wine enthusiast and collector, was brief and positive in his vinous autobiography *Stay Me With Flagons* – 'Krug holds my allegiance as the king of them all; my recollection does not go behind the Krug 1919 but that was truly an excellent wine. And Krug 1928 must be the best wine made in the present century.'

Ian Maxwell Campbell, of course, was the London agent who sold the wine in Britain and, if his opinion is professional, that of his business rival should be even more objective – this comes from *Wayward Tendrils of the Vine*: 'One of my keenest competitors, Henry Rivière, agent for Louis Roederer, and the memory of whose friendship I cherish, came up to me in Mark Lane soon after we had offered the Krug 1928 on the market, and said "Ian I have gone about saying your Krug 1926 is the best champagne ever made and, damn it all, your 1928 is better."'

Michael Broadbent makes the comment – 'Bear in mind that the French like their wines young, whereas the English – or the sophisticated English – like them older, certainly mature – whether champagne, claret, port or whatever. The taste and liking for old champagne – when it has lost much of its *mousse* and is more of a gentle old wine – is peculiarly English.'

Certainly a bottle of the blend of the Ay and Avize 1904 vintage – the year of Joseph II's wedding – of which Paul I laid down a large parcel – was a fine, majestic white wine when Paul Krug opened a bottle at dinner in 1974.

He relates that, in 1959, an Englishman telephoned Jean Seydoux in Reims, to say he had inherited a cellar which contained Krug 1904, 1906, 1911 and 1915 and to enquire whether it was ready to drink and, if so, should he start with the 1904? Yes, he was told, it will be all right to drink it now, it should be good wine and he could drink it in date order. He was content, and it was so.

Evidence of early vintages comes from Walter Berry, visiting Joseph II in the Boulevard Lundy – 'Krug, *Private Cuvée,* 1884, 1900 and 1911; they were all beautiful wines. I have been trying to find a flaw in one of them in order to enhance the description of the others but it cannot be done.'

Krug has a place, too, in the first of all English studies in wine-appreciation, by that erudite scholar and long-experienced drinker, Professor George Saintsbury, in his classic, *Notes on a Cellar Book* – 'Taking well known brands all round, I do not know that I was more faithful to any than to Krug. I began my fancy for it with a [18]'65, which memory represents as being, though dry, that "winy wine", as Thackeray describes it, which champagne ought to be, but too seldom is. And when, just fifty years after that vintage, I drank farewell to my cellar before giving up housekeeping, it was in a bottle of Krug's *Private Cuvée* 1906.'

In a series of meals at Rue Coquebert, the procession of Krug 1904, 1920, the historic 1928 (here is entered a prayer that the writer may taste it once more before he dies), 1929, 1937, 1953, 1955 – in Paul Krug's opinion the best post-war vintage – 1964 and 1966, all educationally intended, proved imaginatively stimulating. To taste them for the first time was a blaze of light on understanding. Those bottles were proffered generously, but with absolute certainty of their eminence.

It was André Simon who wrote – 'Glory is no cheap commodity. No one is more fully aware of this fact than the champagne shipper. His champagne carries his name to the ends of the earth, and wherever he goes, provided he

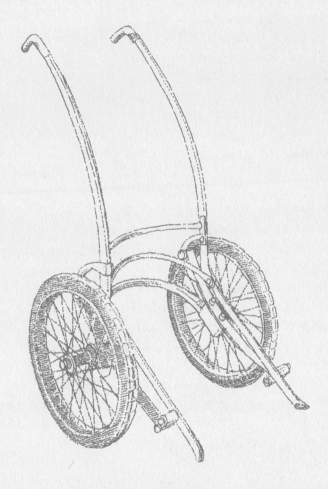

moves in polite society, his name is known and serves as an introduction in a great many quarters. But what of his responsibility? So long as there is a vestige of a label with his name on it left on a bottle he is responsible for the wine within the bottle.' To the Krug family the responsibility is a matter also of pride. That, however, is not sufficient.

Under the economic pressures of the present day it seems that the decision must be taken for Krug to remain the wine of connoisseurs, trusting that they will sustain its viability, or it must compete in the widest market with every other house. Perhaps some compromise will emerge. Success in champagne – indeed, in all wine – depends upon fashion; fashion is a child of its age and so are the men who succeed in those businesses dependent on fashion. The single-minded Joseph from Mainz overcame the handicap of being a stranger to the country and wine of Champagne. The expansive nineteenth-century Edwardian, Paul, rode a wave of success over the obstacles of war, phylloxera, and competition in the main export markets. The dutiful son Joseph saw the business through invasion and occupation in two wars. All those difficulties, however, were either soluble within the world of champagne by methods the Krug *gérants* could achieve; or, like the wars, were, though violent, temporary complications.

The difficulties of Krug now are those of all businesses in the capitalist society of the last part of the twentieth century – a world where the family unit has been hard pressed to survive. That is why, at bottom, Paul Krug II has found himself, force-put, a businessman-politician. It explains why, while it was automatically assumed that Henri and Rémi would follow their father into the business, Henri is by no means positive that his sons will join it when they grow up.

The fifth link has been forged. Its capacity to provide security for a sixth is now being tested.

Henri and Rémi Krug

Acknowledgements

Anyone who writes a book on any aspect of this subject must be deeply indebted to Patrick Forbes's wide-ranging, deeply researched and sympathetic study, *Champagne* (Gollancz, 1967). Thanks are proffered also to Michael Broadbent of Christies' Wine Department for unusual wine scholarship most generously shared; to Brigadier Lorne Campbell of Airds, vc, for guidance, and for permission to quote from *Wayward Tendrils of the Vine,* and *Reminiscences of a Vintner,* both by his father, Ian Maxwell Campbell; to Alec Waugh, Cassell and Co, and A D Peters for the extract from *In Praise of Wine*; to Messrs Michael Joseph, Messrs Constable, and the executors of André Simon for quotations from *In the Twilight* and *Champagne*; to Anthony Berry and Berry Bros and Rudd for the extracts from *In Search of Wine* by C W Berry; to Messrs Michael Joseph and the executors of Maurice Healey for the quotation from *Stay Me With Flagons*; and to the executors of Professor George Saintsbury and Messrs Macmillan and Co for the passage from *Notes on a Cellar Book* by George Saintsbury.

Above all this registers a debt of gratitude for guidance, information and hospitality to Paul II, Jacqueline, Henri and Rémi Krug; and, for the valuable facts derived from their immaculate figures, the late Messrs Lutz and Koch.

Glossary

andouillettes sausages of pork chitterlings.

Appellation Contrôlée the generally used term for *Appellation d'Origine Contrôlée* which allows wines made from specific grapes, in the prescribed fashion, and to a stipulated yield per hectare, to bear the name of the region, district, commune or vineyard where they are produced.

arbanne a grape type permitted, but rarely used, in the making of champagne.

biscuit de Reims a vanilla-flavoured biscuit made in Reims traditionally to be dipped in champagne or coffee and then eaten.

blanc de blancs white wine made from white grapes only.

blanc de noirs white wine made from black grapes only, by removal of the skins before they can tint the must.

boucheur the man who inserts and, in the case of champagne, hammers, the cork into the neck of the bottle.

bourgeois château usually a Bordeaux wine *château* of the class below the 'classed' of 'classified' growths.

brut (or *nature*) strictly speaking a naturally completely dry wine; of champagne it usually means, in practice, one with minimal *dosage* or sweetening.

cassoulet a haricot bean stew made with pork, mutton and goose or duck, originally in an earthenware vessel called a *cassole d'Issan*.

cépage grape variety.

chai term used in Bordeaux for the store or cellar where wines are kept.

La Champagne the province of Champagne.

La Champagne viticole the winefield of Champagne.

le champagne the sparkling wine of Champagne.

les Champenois the people of the province of Champagne.

charcuterie pork butchery.

chardonnay a type of white grape, often called *pinot chardonnay* but not in fact a *pinot*: it is used for champagne and the fine white wines of Burgundy.

chef de cave a cellar-master.

collerette or *cravate* the neck-label of a bottle.

Coteaux Champenois still wine produced in *la Champagne viticole*, formerly called *vin nature de la Champagne*.

cravate or *collerette* the neck-label of a bottle.

crémant or 'creaming' wine, a white wine made – sometimes in Champagne – from white and black grapes, but less sparkling and lighter than champagne.

cru strictly a growth; a term used for the output of a particular vineyard, usually a fine one.

'crus non cotés' used in Champagne of the lower-priced growths of the Marne vineyards.

cuvée basically it means a vatting of wine; but, in Champagne *première cuvée* – like *tête de cuvée* in Burgundy – means the product of the first pressing of the grapes.

cuve close method of making sparkling wine invented by Eugene Charmat (and sometimes called the Charmat process) in which wine is artificially fermented, aged, and clarified under pressure in a series of tanks.

dégorgement 'disgorging', the extraction of a champagne cork and the deposit which has settled on it during the process of *remuage*, before the second cork is inserted.

dégorgeur the man who disgorges the champagne bottle.

demi-sec (or *goût Français*) a half-dry champagne; somewhat too sweet for the general British taste.

dosage the addition of wine and sugar to a bottle of champagne to make good the loss caused by *dégorgement* and to give it the desired degree of sweetness.

doux of a wine, sweet.

en cercles of wines, in barrel.

épluchage the picking out of rotten grapes.

fraudeurs defrauders.

gérant manager.

goût Americain of champagne, slightly sweeter than *goût Anglais*.

goût Anglais of champagne, dry.

goût Français of champagne, fairly sweet.

grande marque of champagne it means the leading houses. There is no strict classification; certainly, however, the twelve champagne houses who established the Champagne Academy are entitled to the description.

gros plant doré d'Ay a black grape, variant of the *pinot noir*, produced outstandingly in the vineyards of Ay.

jambon de Reims or *jambonneau* a local speciality, ham cooked with green herbs and breadcrumbs which form vein-like green lines in the meat.

liqueur de tirage the liquor, composed of the same wine, plus some sugar, added to the champagne in the bottling vat to ensure adequate effervescence during the secondary fermentation.

liqueur d'expédition the liquor, composed of the same wine plus sugar, that is added to champagne – in *dosage* – before the final corking to make good volume lost in *dégorgement* and to give it the desired degree of sweetness.

logis gate lodge.

maie the oak press traditionally used for pressing grapes in Champagne.

manipulants in Champagne, members of the wine-making houses.

marcassin a young wild boar.

matelote a fish stew made with wine.

mélange blend.

méthode champenoise the method employed to make sparkling wine in Champagne and some other areas.

mousse of a sparkling wine, foam.

mousseux a sparkling wine.

must freshly pressed grapes.

négociant in wine production, a dealer in wines or grapes.

Négociant Manipulant in champagne, the identification, by the letters NM, of a bottle-label as that of the actual maker of the champagne.

'*Oeil de Perdrix*' literally 'eye of a partridge'; term sometimes used to describe a *rosé* or pinkish-tinged wine.

Ouverture des Vendanges the announcement of the date – decided by the *Préfet* – on which the grape-harvest may begin.

pâté de grives strictly, a pie of minced or chopped meat of thrush.

pétillant of a wine, slightly sparkling.

petit meslier a delicately flavoured white grape permitted to be used in champagne.

pinot the family name of a group of noble wine-grapes.

pinot blanc the classical white grape of Champagne and the white wines of Burgundy.

pinot meunier a variant of the *pinot noir* important in the making of champagne.

pinot noir the black grape used in the making of champagne and of the fine red burgundies.

potée Champenoise a traditional Champagne dish, a casserole of mixed meats, sausages and vegetables.

prix de base basic price (for grapes); actually the top or 100 per cent price on which that for other, lower qualities is based.

prix du raisin the list of graded prices to be paid for the different grapes of a champagne vintage.

pupître literally, a desk; in champagne-making, the sloping boards, into which are cut the elliptical holes in which champagne bottles are turned during *remuage*.

rebèche the fourth pressing of champagne grapes; it must not be included in champagne.

récoltants-manipulants grape-growers who make and sell their own champagne.

remuage the process of shaking and turning champagne bottles in elliptical holes until they stand cork downwards so that the deposit settles on the cork.

remueur the cellar worker who carries out *remuage*.

rivière river.

sec (or *goût Américain*) literally, dry; of champagne, less dry than *brut*.

serre a pressing of grapes.

sur pointe on its tip – said of a champagne bottle at the end of the process of *remuage*.

sous marques the lesser wines of a champagne house.

table de gibier game table.

taille the three last pressings of champagne grapes after the first (*vin de cuvée*): the first two may be used in champagne, the third (*rebèche*) may not.

tirage the bottling of champagne.

vendange the harvest of wine grapes.

vendangeurs the grape harvesters.

ventes sur place sold on the premises.

vigneron a wine-grower.

vignoble a vineyard or wine-growing district.

vin de cru wine made from the grapes of a single vineyard.

vin de cuvée the juice extracted from the grapes at the first pressing.

vin nature de la Champagne formerly the official name for still wine of Champagne, altered in 1974 to *Coteaux Champenois*.

vin ordinaire ordinary, undistinguished, country wine.

Bibliography

BERRY, C W *A Miscellany of Wine*, Constable, London 1932
   Viniana, Constable, London 1934
   In Search of Wine, Constable, London 1935

BROADBENT, Michael (editor) *Christie's Wine Review 1972*, Christie's, London
   Christie's Wine Review 1973, Christie's, London
   Christie's Wine Review 1974, Christie's, London

CAMPBELL, Ian Maxwell *Reminiscences of a Vintner*, Chapman & Hall, London
   Wayward Tendrils of the Vine, Chapman & Hall, London 1948

CARTER, Youngman *Drinking Champagne and Brandy*, Hamish Hamilton, London 1968

DION, Roger *Histoire de la Vigne et du Vin de France*, Paris 1959

DISHER, M Willson *Winkles and Champagne*, Batsford, London 1938

DUTTON, Ralph and HOLDEN, Lord *The Land of France*, Batsford, London 1952

FORBES, Patrick *Champagne*, Gollancz, London 1967

HEALY, Maurice *Stay Me With Flagons*, Michael Joseph, London 1949

HYAMS, Edward *Vin*, Newnes, London 1959

JOHNSON, Hugh *World Atlas of Wine*, Mitchell Beazley, London 1971

KAUFMAN, William *Champagne*, André Deutsch, London 1973

LEGRAND, Napoleon E *Champagne*, Malot-Braine, Reims 1897

LICHINE, Alexis *Wines of France*, Cassell, London 1953, 1956

MACQUEEN-POPE, W *The Melodies Linger On*, W H Allen, London 1950

MENDELSOHN, Oscar *The Earnest Drinker*, Allen & Unwin, London 1950

NOWELL-SMITH, Simon *Edwardian England 1901–1914*, Oxford University Press, London 1964

ORDISH, George *The Great Wine Blight*, Dent, London 1972

RAY, Cyril *Bollinger*, Davies, London 1971
In a Glass Lightly, Methuen, London 1967

REDDING, Cyrus *A History and Description of Modern Wines*, Whittaker, London 1836

SAINTSBURY, George *Notes on a Cellar Book*, Macmillan, London 1920

SCHOONMAKER, Frank and MARVEL, Tom *The Complete Wine Book*, Routledge, London 1935

SCOTT, J M *Vineyards of France*, Hodder & Stoughton, London 1950

SHAND, P Morton *A Book of French Wines*, Cape, London 1928

SIMON, André L *History of the Wine Trade in England*, Wyman, London 1906–1909
In Vino Veritas, Richards, London 1913
Champagne, Constable, London 1934
A Wine Primer, Michael Joseph, London 1946
By Request, Wine and Food Society, London 1957
The Noble Grapes and the Great Wines of France, George Rainbird, London 1957
A History of Champagne, Ebury Press, London 1962
In the Twilight, Michael Joseph, London 1969

VIZETELLY, Henry *Facts about Champagne and other Sparkling Wines*, Vizetelly, London 1879

WAUGH, Alec *In Praise of Wine*, Cassell, London 1959

YOUNGER, William *Gods, Men and Wine*, Michael Joseph, London 1966

Index

Compiled by Anna Pavord